MUIRHEAD LIBRARY OF PHILOSOPHY

AN admirable statement of the aims of the Library of Philosophy was provided by the first editor, the late Professor J. H. Muirhead, in his description of the original programme printed in Erdmann's *History of Philosophy* under the date 1890. This was slightly modified in subsequent volumes to take the form of the following statement:

'The Muirhead Library of Philosophy was designed as a contribution to the History of Modern Philosophy under the heads: first of different Schools of Thought—Sensationalist, Realist, Idealist, Intuitivist; secondly of different Subjects—Psychology, Ethics, Aesthetics, Political Philosophy, Theology. While much had been done in England in tracing the course of evolution in nature, history, economics, morals and religion, little had been done in tracing the development of thought on these subjects. Yet "the evolution of opinion is part of the whole evolution".

'By the co-operation of different writers in carrying out this plan it was hoped that a thoroughness and completeness of treatment, otherwise unattainable, might be secured. It was believed also that from writers mainly British and American fuller consideration of English Philosophy than it had hitherto received might be looked for. In the earlier series of books containing, among others, Bosanquet's *History of Aesthetic*, Pfleiderer's *Rational Theology since Kant*, Albee's *History of English Utilitarianism*, Bonar's *Philosophy and Political Economy*, Brett's *History of Psychology*, Ritchie's *Natural Rights*, these objects were to a large extent effected.

'In the meantime original work of a high order was being produced both in England and America by such writers as Bradley, Stout, Bertrand Russell, Baldwin, Urban, Montague, and others, and a new interest in foreign works, German, French and Italian, which had either become classical or were attracting public attention, had developed. The scope of the Library thus became extended into something more international, and it is entering on the fifth decade of its existence in the hope that it may contribute to that mutual understanding between countries which is so pressing a need of the present time.'

The need which Professor Muirhead stressed is no less pressing today, and few will deny that philosophy has much to do with enabling us to meet it, although no one, least of all Muirhead himself, would regard that as the sole, or even the main, object of philosophy. As Professor Muirhead continues to lend the distinction of his name to the Library of Philosophy it seemed not inappropriate to allow him to recall us to these aims in his own words. The emphasis on the history of thought also seemed to me very timely; and the number of important works promised for the Library in the near future augur well for the continued fulfilment, in this and other ways, of the expectations of the original editor.

H. D. LEWIS

a

MUIRHEAD LIBRARY OF PHILOSOPHY

General Editor: Professor H. D. Lewis

Professor of History and Philosophy of Religion in the University of London

Muirhead Library of Philosophy

TIME AND FREE WILL

by HENRI BERGSON
MATTER AND MEMORY

HENRI BERGSON

TIME AND FREE WILL

An Essay on the Immediate Data
of Consciousness

Authorised Translation by

F. L. POGSON

M.A.

LONDON: GEORGE ALLEN & UNWIN LTD
NEW YORK: THE MACMILLAN COMPANY

FIRST PUBLISHED IN 1910
SECOND IMPRESSION 1912
THIRD IMPRESSION 1913
FOURTH IMPRESSION 1921
FIFTH IMPRESSION 1928
SIXTH IMPRESSION 1950
SEVENTH IMPRESSION 1959

Καὶ εἴ τις δὲ τὴν φύσιν ἔροιτο τινσς ἕνεκα ποιεῖ
εἰ τοῦ ἐρωτῶντος ἐθέλοι ἐπαΐειν καὶ λέγειν, εἴποι
ἄν· "ἐχρῆν μὲν μὴ ἐρωτᾶν, ἀλλὰ συνιέναι καὶ αὐτὸν
σιωπῇ, ὥυπερ ἐγὼ σιωπῶ καὶ οὐκ εἴθισμαι λέγειν."

PLOTINUS.

PRINTED IN GREAT BRITAIN
BY NEILL AND CO. LTD., EDINBURGH

TRANSLATOR'S PREFACE

HENRI LOUIS BERGSON was born in Paris, October
18, 1859. He entered the École normale in
1878, and was admitted agrégé de philosophie
in 1881 and docteur ès lettres in 1889. After
holding professorships in various provincial and
Parisian lycées, he became maître de conférences
at the École normale supérieure in 1897, and
since 1900 has been professor at the Collège de
France. In 1901 he became a member of the
Institute on his election to the Académie des
Sciences morales et politiques.

A full list of Professor Bergson's works is given
in the appended bibliography. In making the
following translation of his *Essai sur les données
immédiates de la conscience* I have had the great
advantage of his co-operation at every stage,
and the aid which he has given has been most
generous and untiring. The book itself was
worked out and written during the years 1883
to 1887 and was originally published in 1889.
The foot-notes in the French edition contain a
certain number of references to French translations of English works. In the present translation I am responsible for citing these references
from the original English. This will account

for the fact that editions are sometimes referred
to which have appeared subsequently to 1889.
I have also added fairly extensive marginal
summaries and a full index.

In France the *Essai* is already in its seventh
edition. Indeed, one of the most striking facts
about Professor Bergson's works is the extent
to which they have appealed not only to the
professional philosophers, but also to the ordinary
cultivated public. The method which he pursues
is not the conceptual and abstract method which
has been the dominant tradition in philosophy.
For him reality is not to be reached by any
elaborate construction of thought : it is given
in immediate experience as a flux, a continuous
process of becoming, to be grasped by intuition,
by sympathetic insight. Concepts break up the
continuous flow of reality into parts external to
one another, they further the interests of language
and social life and are useful primarily for practical purposes. But they give us nothing of the
life and movement of reality ; rather, by substituting for this an artificial reconstruction, a
patchwork of dead fragments, they lead to the
difficulties which have always beset the intellectualist philosophy, and which on its premises
are insoluble. Instead of attempting a solution
in the intellectualist sense, Professor Bergson
calls upon his readers to put these broken fragments of reality behind them, to immerse themselves in the living stream of things and to

find their difficulties swept away in its resistless flow.

In the present volume Professor Bergson first deals with the intensity of conscious states. He shows that quantitative differences are applicable only to magnitudes, that is, in the last resort, to space, and that intensity in itself is purely qualitative. Passing then from the consideration of separate conscious states to their multiplicity, he finds that there are two forms of multiplicity : quantitative or discrete multiplicity involves the intuition of space, but the multiplicity of conscious states is wholly qualitative. This unfolding multiplicity constitutes duration, which is a succession without distinction, an interpenetration of elements so heterogeneous that former states can never recur. The idea of a homogeneous and measurable time is shown to be an artificial concept, formed by the intrusion of the idea of space into the realm of pure duration. Indeed, the whole of Professor Bergson's philosophy centres round his conception of *real concrete duration* and the specific *feeling* of duration which our consciousness has when it does away with convention and habit and gets back to its natural attitude. At the root of most errors in philosophy he finds a confusion between this *concrete duration* and the *abstract time* which mathematics, physics, and even language and common sense, substitute for it. Applying these results to the problem of free will, he shows that the difficulties arise from taking up one's stand *after* the act has been performed, and applying the conceptual method to it. From the point of view of the living, developing self these difficulties are shown to be illusory, and freedom, though not definable in abstract or conceptual terms, is declared to be one of the clearest facts established by observation.

It is no doubt misleading to attempt to sum up a system of philosophy in a sentence, but perhaps some part of the spirit of Professor Bergson's philosophy may be gathered from the motto which, with his permission, I have prefixed to this translation :—" If a man were to inquire of Nature the reason of her creative activity, and if she were willing to give ear and answer, she would say—' Ask me not, but understand in silence, even as I am silent and am not wont to speak.' "

F. L. POGSON.

OXFORD,
June, 1910.

BIBLIOGRAPHY

I. WORKS BY BERGSON.

    (a) *Books.*

Quid Aristoteles de loco senserit, (Thesis), Paris, 1889.

Essai sur les données immédiates de la conscience, Paris, 1889, 1910.[7]

Matière et Mémoire, Essai sur la relation du corps avec l'esprit, Paris, 1896, 1910.[6]

Le Rire, Essai sur la signification du comique, Paris, 1900, 1910.[6] (First published in the *Revue de Paris*, 1900, Vol. I., pp. 512–545 and 759–791.)

L'Evolution créatrice, Paris, 1907, 1910.[6]

    (b) *Articles.*

La Spécialité. (Address at the distribution of prizes at the lycée of Angers, Aug. 1882.)

De la simulation inconsciente dans l'état d'hypnotisme. *Revue philosophique*, Vol. 22, 1886, pp. 525–531.

Le bon sens et les études classiques. (Address at the distribution of prizes at the " Concours général des lycées et collèges," 1895.)

Mémoire et reconnaissance. (*Revue philos.* Mar., Apr. 1896, pp. 225–248 and 380–399. Republished in *Matière et Mémoire.*)

Perception et matière. (*Rev. de Mét. et de Mor.* May 1896, pp. 257–277. Republished in *Matière et Mémoire.*)

Note sur les origines psychologiques de notre croyance à la loi de causalité. (Lecture at the Philosophical Congress in Paris, 1900, published in the *Bibliothèque du Congrès International de Philosophie ;* cf. *Revue de Métaphysique et de Morale*, Sept. 1900, pp. 655 ff.)

Le Rêve. (Lecture at the *Institut psychologique international :* published in the *Bulletin de l'Institut psych. intern.* May 1901 ; cf. *Revue scientifique*, 4° S., Vol. 15, June 8, 1901, pp. 705–713, and *Revue de Philosophie*, June 1901, pp. 486–488.)

Le Parallélisme psycho-physique et la métaphysique positive. *Bulletin de la Société française de Philosophie,* June 1901.

L'Effort intellectuel. *Revue philosophique,* Jan. 1902.

Introduction à la métaphysique. *Revue de Mét. et de Mor.* Jan. 1903.

Le Paralogisme psycho-physiologique. (Lecture at the Philosophical Congress in Geneva, 1904, published in the *Revue de Mét. et de Mor.* Nov. 1904, pp. 895–908 ; see also pp. 1027–1036.)

L'Idée de néant, *Rev. philos.* Nov. 1906, pp. 449–466. (Part of Chap. 4 of *L'Évolution créatrice.*)

Notice sur la vie et les œuvres de M. Félix Ravaisson-Mollien. (Lecture before the Académie des Sciences morales et politiques : published in the *Proceedings* of the Academy, Vol. 25, pp. 1 ff. Paris, 1907.)

Le Souvenir du présent et la fausse reconnaissance. *Rev. philos.* Dec. 1908, pp. 561–593.

(c) *Miscellaneous.*

Lucrèce : Extraits . . . avec une étude sur la poésie, la philosophie, la physique, le texte et la langue de Lucrèce. Paris, 1884.

Principes de métaphysique et de psychologie d'après M. Paul Janet. *Revue philos.,* Vol. 44, Nov. 1897, pp. 525–551.

Collaboration au *Vocabulaire philosophique, Bulletin de la Soc. fr. de Phil.* July 1902, Aug. 1907, Aug. 1908, Aug. 1909.

Remarques sur la place et le caractère de la Philosophie dans l'Enseignement secondaire, *Bulletin de la Soc. fr. de Phil.* Feb. 1903, pp. 44 ff.

Remarques sur la notion de la liberté morale, *Bulletin de la Soc. fr. de Phil.* Apr. 1903, pp. 101–103.

Remarques à propos de la philosophie sociale de Cournot, *Bulletin de la Soc. fr. de Phil.* Aug. 1903, p. 229.

Préface de la *Psychologie rationnelle* de M. Lubac, Paris, Alcan, 1904.

Sur sa relation à W. James, *Revue philosophique,* Vol. 60, 1905, p. 229 f.

Sur sa théorie de la perception, *Bulletin de la Soc. fr. de Philos.* Mar. 1905, pp. 94 ff.

Rapport sur le concours pour le prix Bordin, 1905, ayant pour sujet Maine de Biran. (*Mémoires de l'Académie des Sciences morales et politiques*, Vol. 25, pp. 809 ff. Paris, 1907.)

Rapport sur le concours pour le prix Le Dissez de Penanrun, 1907. (*Mémoires de l'Académie des Sciences morales et politiques*, Vol. 26, pp. 771 ff. Paris, 1909.)

Sur l'*Évolution créatrice*, *Revue du Mois*, Sept. 1907, p. 351.

A propos de l'évolution de l'intelligence géométrique, *Revue de Mét. et de Mor.* Jan. 1908, pp. 28–33.

Sur l'influence de sa philosophie sur les élèves des lycées, *Bulletin de la Soc. fr. de Philos.*, Jan. 1908, p. 21 ; cf. *L'Année psychologique*, 1908, pp. 229–231.

Réponse à une enquête sur la question religieuse (*La Question religieuse* par Frédéric Charpin, Paris, 1908).

Remarques sur l'organisation des Congrès de Philosophie. *Bulletin de la Soc. fr. de Phil.* Jan. 1909, p. 11 f.

Préface à un volume de la collection *Les grands philosophes*, (*G. Tarde*, par ses fils). Paris. Michaud, 1909.

Remarques à propos d'une thèse soutenue par M. Dwelshauvers " L'inconscient dans la vie mentale." *Bulletin de la Soc. fr. de Phil.*, Feb. 1910.

A propos d'un article de Mr. W. B. Pitkin intitulé " James and Bergson." *Journal of Philosophy, Psychology and Scientific Methods*, Vol. VII, No. 14, July 7, 1910, pp. 385–388.

II. SELECT LIST OF BOOKS AND ARTICLES DEALING IN WHOLE OR IN PART WITH BERGSON AND HIS PHILOSOPHY.

(Arranged alphabetically under each language.)

S. *Alexander*, *Matière et Mémoire*, (*Mind*, Oct. 1897, pp. 572–3).

B. H. *Bode*, *L'Évolution créatrice*, (*Philosophical Review*, 1908, pp. 84–89).

W. *Boyd*, *L'Évolution créatrice*, (*Review of Theology and Philosophy*, Oct. 1907, pp. 249–251).

H. *Wildon Carr*, Bergson's Theory of Knowledge, (*Proceedings of the Aristotelian Society*, London, 1909. New Series, Vol. IX, pp. 41–60).

H. *Wildon Carr*, Bergson's Theory of Instinct, (*Proceedings of the Aristotelian Society*, London, 1910, N.S., Vol. X).

H. Wildon Carr, The Philosophy of Bergson, (*Hibbert Journal*, July 1910, pp. 873–883).

W. J. Ferrar, L'Évolution créatrice, (*Commonwealth*, Dec. 1909, pp. 364–367).

H. N. Gardiner, Mémoire et reconnaissance, (*Psychological Review*, 1896, pp. 578–580).

T. E. Hulme, The New Philosophy, (*New Age*, July 1, 29, 1909).

William James, A Pluralistic Universe, London, 1909, pp. 225–273.

William James, The Philosophy of Bergson, (*Hibbert Journal*, April 1909, pp. 562–577. Reprinted in *A Pluralistic Universe ;* see above).

William James, Bradley or Bergson ? (*Journal of Philosophy, Psychology and Scientific Methods*, Vol. VII, No. 2, Jan. 20, 1910, pp. 29–33).

H. M. Kallen, James, Bergson and Mr. Pitkin, (*Journal of Philosophy, Psychology and Scientific Methods*, June 23, 1910, pp. 353–357).

A. Lalande, Philosophy in France, 1907, (*Philosophical Review*, May, 1908).

J. A. Leighton, On Continuity and Discreteness, (*Journal of Philosophy, Psychology and Scientific Methods*, Apr. 28, 1910, pp. 231–238).

T. Loveday, L'Évolution créatrice, (*Mind*, July 1908, pp. 402–8).

A. O. Lovejoy, The Metaphysician of the Life-Force, (*Nation*, New York, Sept. 30, 1909).

A. Mitchell, L'Évolution créatrice, (*Journal of Philosophy, Psychology and Scientific Methods*, Vol. V, No. 22, Oct. 22, 1908, pp. 603–612).

W. Scott Palmer, Presence and Omnipresence, (*Contemporary Review*, June 1908, pp. 734–742).

W. Scott Palmer, Thought and Instinct, (*Nation*, June 5, 1909).

W. Scott Palmer, Life and the Brain, (*Contemporary Review*, Oct., 1909, pp. 474–484).

W. B. Pitkin, James and Bergson ; or, Who is against Intellect ? (*Journal of Philosophy, Psychology and Scientific Methods*, Apr. 28, 1910, pp. 225–231).

G. R. T. Ross, A New Theory of Laughter, (*Nation*, Nov. 28, 1908).

G. R. T. Ross, The Philosophy of Vitalism, (*Nation*, Mar. 13, 1909).

J. Royce, The Reality of the Temporal, (*Int. Journal of Ethics*, Apr. 1910, pp. 257-271).

G. M. Sauvage, The New Philosophy in France, (*Catholic University Bulletin*, Washington, Apr. 1906, Mar. 1908).

Norman Smith, Subjectivism and Realism in Modern Philosophy, (*Philosophical Review*, Apr. 1908, pp. 138-148).

G. F. Stout, Free Will and Determinism, (*Speaker*, London, May 10, 1890).

J. H. Tufts, Humor, (*Psychological Review*, 1901, pp. 98-99).

G. Tyrrell, Creative Evolution, (*Hibbert Journal*, Jan. 1908, pp. 435-442).

T. Whittaker, Essai sur les données immédiates de la conscience, (*Mind*, Apr. 1890, pp. 292-3).

G. Aimel, Individualisme et philosophie bergsonienne, (*Revue de Philos.*, June 1908).

Balthasar, Le problème de Dieu d'après la philosophie nouvelle, (*Revue néo-scolastique*, Nov. 1907).

G. Batault, La philosophie de M. Bergson, (*Mercure de France*, Mar. 16, 1908, pp. 193-211).

G. Belot, Une théorie nouvelle de la liberté, (*Revue philosophique*, Vol. XXX, 1890, pp. 360-392).

G. Belot, Un nouveau spiritualisme, Matière et Mémoire, (*Rev. philos.* Vol. XLIV, 1897, pp. 183-199).

Jean Blum, La philosophie de M. Bergson et la poésie symboliste, (*Mercure de France*, Sept. 15, 1906).

C. Bouglé, Syndicalistes et Bergsoniens, (*Revue du Mois*, Apr. 1909, pp. 403-416).

G. Cantecor, La philosophie nouvelle et la vie de l'esprit, (*Rev. philos.* Mar. 1903, pp. 252-277).

P. Cérésole, Le parallélisme psycho-physiologique et l'argument de M. Bergson, (*Archives de Psychologie*, Vol. V, Oct. 1905, pp. 112-120).

A. Chaumeix, La philosophie de M. Bergson, (*Journal des Débats*, May 24, 1908. Reprinted in *Pragmatisme et Modernisme*, Paris, Alcan, 1909).

A. Chaumeix, Les critiques du rationalisme, (*Revue Hebdomadaire,* Paris, Jan. 1, 1910, pp. 1–33).

A. Chide, Le mobilisme moderne, Paris, Alcan, 1908. (See also *Revue philos.,* Apr. 1908, Dec. 1909).

C. Coignet, Kant et Bergson, (*Revue Chrétienne,* July 1904).

C. Coignet, La vie d'après M. Bergson, (*Bericht über den III Kongress für Philosophie,* Heidelberg, 1909, pp. 358–364).

L. Constant, Cours de M. Bergson sur l'histoire de l'idée de temps, (*Revue de Philos.* Jan. 1904, pp. 105–111. Summary of lectures).

P. L. Couchoud, La métaphysique nouvelle, à propos de *Matière et Mémoire* de M. Bergson, (*Revue de Métaphysique et de Morale,* Mar. 1902, pp. 225–243).

L. Couturat, La théorie du temps de Bergson, (*Rev. de Mét. et de Mor.* 1896, pp. 646–669).

Léon Cristiani, Le problème de Dieu et le pragmatisme, Paris, Bloud et Cie., 1908.

F. Le Dantec, L'Évolution créatrice, (*Revue du Mois,* Aug. 1907. Reprinted in *Science et Conscience,* Paris, Flammarion, 1908).

L. Dauriac, Le Rire, (*Revue philos.* Dec. 1900, pp. 665–670).

V. Delbos, Matière et Mémoire, (*Rev. de Mét. et de Mor.* May 1897, pp. 353–389).

G. L. Duprat, La spatialité des faits psychiques, (*Rev. philos.,* May 1907, pp. 492–501).

G. Dwelshauvers, Raison et Intuition, Étude sur la philosophie de M. Bergson, (*La Belgique artistique et littéraire,* Nov. Dec. 1905, Apr. 1906).

G. Dwelshauvers, M. Bergson et la méthode intuitive, (*Revue du Mois,* Sept. 1907, pp. 336–350).

G. Dwelshauvers, De l'intuition dans l'acte de l'esprit, (*Rev. de Mét. et de Mor.* Jan. 1908, pp. 55–65).

A. Farges, Le problème de la contingence d'après M. Bergson, (*Revue pratique d'apologétique,* Apr. 15, 1909).

A. Farges, L'erreur fondamentale de la philosophie nouvelle, (*Revue thomiste,* May–June, 1909).

A. Farges, Théorie fondamentale de l'acte, avec la critique de la philosophie nouvelle de M. Bergson, Paris, Berche et Tralin, 1909.

Alfred Fouillée, Le mouvement idéaliste et la réaction contre la science positive, Paris, Alcan, 1896, pp. 198–206.

Fr. Garrigou-Lagrange, Le sens commun, la philosophie de l'être et les formules dogmatiques, Paris, Beauchesne, 1909.

Jules de Gaultier, Le réalisme du continu, (*Revue philos.*, Jan. 1910, pp. 39–64).

René Gillouin, Henri Bergson, Paris, 1910. (A volume in the series *Les grands philosophes*).

A. Hollard, L'Évolution créatrice, (*Foi et Vie*, Sept. 16, 1907, pp. 545–550).

B. Jacob, La philosophie d'hier et celle d'aujourd'hui, (*Rev. de Mét. et de Mor.* Mar. 1898, pp. 170–201).

G. Lechalas, Le nombre et le temps dans leurs rapports avec l'espace, (*Ann. de Phil. chrét.* N.S. Vol. 22, 1890, pp. 516–540).

G. Lechalas, Matière et Mémoire, (*Ann. de Phil. chrét.* N.S. Vol. 36, 1897, pp. 149–164 and 314–334).

A. Joussain, Romantisme et Religion, Paris, Alcan, 1910.

Legendre, M. Bergson et son *Evolution créatrice*, (*Bulletin de la Semaine*, May 6, 1908).

Lenoble, L'Evolution créatrice, (*Revue du Clergé français*, Jan., 1908).

E. Le Roy, Science et Philosophie, (A Series of articles in the *Rev. de Mét. et de Mor.* 1899 and 1900).

L. Lévy-Bruhl, L'Essai sur les données immédiates de la conscience, (*Rev. philos.*, Vol. 29, 1890, pp. 519–538).

G. H. Luquet, Idées générales de psychologie, Paris, 1906.

J. Lux, Nos philosophes, M. Henri Bergson, (*Revue Bleue*, Dec. 1, 1906).

X. Moisant, La notion de multiplicité dans la philosophie de M. Bergson, (*Revue de Philos.*, June, 1902).

X. Moisant, Dieu dans la philosophie de M. Bergson, (*Revue de Philos.*, May, 1905).

G. Mondain, Remarques sur la théorie matérialiste, (*Foi et Vie*, June 15, 1908, pp. 369–373).

D. Parodi, Le Rire, par H. Bergson, (*Rev. de Mét. et de Mor.* Mar. 1901, pp. 224–236).

T. M. Pègues L'Évolution créatrice (*Revue thomiste*, May-June 1908, pp. 137–163).

C. *Piat*, De l'insuffisance des philosophies de l'intuition, Paris, 1908.

Maurice Pradines, Principes de toute philosophie de l'action, Paris, 1910.

G. *Rageot*, L'Évolution créatrice, (*Rev. philos.*, July 1907). Reprinted and enlarged in *Les savants et la philosophie*, Paris, Alcan, 1907.

F. *Rauh*, La conscience du devenir, (*Rev. de Mét. et de Mor.* Nov. 1897, pp. 659–681, and Jan. 1898, pp. 38–60).

F. *Rauh*, Sur la position du problème du libre arbitre, (*Rev. de Mét. et de Mor.* Nov. 1904, pp. 977–1006).

P. P. *Raymond*, La philosophie de l'intuition et la philosophie du concept, (*Études franciscaines*, June 1909).

E. *Seillière*, L'Allemagne et la philosophie bergsonienne, (*L'Opinion*, July 3, 1909).

G. *Sorel*, L'Évolution créatrice, (*Le Mouvement socialiste*, Oct. Dec. 1907, Jan. Mar. Apr. 1908).

T. *Steeg*, Henri Bergson : Notice biographique avec portrait, (*Revue universelle*, Jan. 1902, pp. 15–16).

J. *de Tonquébec*, La notion de la vérité dans la philosophie nouvelle, Paris, 1908.

J. *de Tonquébec*, Comment interpréter l'ordre du monde à propos du dernier ouvrage de M. Bergson, Paris, Beauchesne, 1908.

H. *Trouche*, L'Évolution créatrice, (*Revue de Philos.* Nov.1908).

H. *Villassère*, L'Évolution créatrice, (*Bulletin critique*, Sept. 1908, pp. 392–411).

Tancrède de Visan, La philosophie de M. Bergson et le lyrisme contemporain, (*Vers et Prose*, Vol. XXI, 1910, pp. 125–140).

L. *Weber*, L'Évolution créatrice, (*Rev. de Mét. et de Mor.* Sept. 1907, pp. 620–670).

V. *Wilbois*, L'esprit positif, (A series of articles in the *Rev. de Mét. et de Mor.* 1900 and 1901).

I. *Benrubi*, Henri Bergson, (*Die Zukunft*, June 4, 1910).·

K. *Bornhausen*, Die Philosophie Henri Bergsons und ihre Bedeutung für den Religionsbegriff, (*Zeitschrift für Theologie und Kirche*, Tübingen, Jahrg. XX, Heft 1 1910, pp. 39–77.

O. Braun, Materie und Gedächtnis, (Archiv für die gesamte Psychologie, Vol. 15, 1909, Heft 4, pp. 13–15).

Hans Driesch, H. Bergson, der biologische Philosoph., *(Zeitschrift für den Ausbau der Entwickelungslehre*, Jahrg. II, Heft 1/2, Stuttgart, 1908).

V. Eschbach, Henri Bergson, *(Kölnische Volkszeitung*, Jan. 20, 1910).

Giessler, Le Rêve, *(Zeitschrift für Psychologie und Physiologie der Sinnesorgane*, Vol. 29, 1902, p. 231).

J. Goldstein, Henri Bergson und der Zeitlosigkeitsidealismus, *(Frankfurter Zeitung*, May 2, 1909).

J. Goldstein, Henri Bergson und die Sozialwissenschaft, *(Archiv für Sozialwissenschaft und Sozialpolitik*, Bd. XXXI, Heft 1, July 1910, pp. 1–22).

A. Gurewitsch, Die französische Metaphysik der Gegenwart *(Archiv für system. Philos.* Bd. IX, Heft 4, Nov. 1903, pp. 462–490).

Heymans, Le Rire, *(Zeitsch. f. Psychol. u. Physiol. d. Sinnesorgane*, Vol. 25, 1901, pp. 155–6).

K. Joël, Neues Denken, *(Neue Rundschau*, Apr. 1910, pp. 549–558).

H. von Keyserling, Bergson, *(Allgemeine Zeitung*, München, Nov. 28, 1908).

R. Kroner, Henri Bergson, *(Logos*, Bd. I, Heft 1, Tübingen, 1910).

*A.Lasson,*H.Bergson,*(Deutsche Literaturzeitung,*May28,1910).

R. Müller-Freienfels, *Materie und Gedächtnis*, *(Zeitsch. f. Psychol. u. Physiol. d. Sinnesorgane*, May 1910, Vol. 56, Heft 1/2, pp. 126–129).

A. Pilzecker, Mémoire et reconnaissance, *(Zeitsch. f. Psychol., u. Physiol. d. Sinnesorgane*, Vol. 13, 1897, pp. 229–232).

Hans Prager, Henri Bergsons metaphysische Grundanschauung, *(Archiv für system. Philos.* 1910, Bd. XVI, Heft 3, pp. 310–320).

G. Seliber, Der Pragmatismus und seine Gegner, *(Archiv für system. Philos.* 1909, pp. 287–298).

A. Steenbergen, Henri Bergsons Intuitive Philosophie, Jena, 1909.

W. Windelband, Preface to *Materie und Gedächtnis*, Jena, 1908, pp. I–XV.

Th. Ziehen, Matière et Mémoire, (Zeitschrift für Philosophie und philos. Kritik, Dec. 1898, pp. 295–299).

Roberto Ardigò, Una pretesa pregiudiziale contro il posi tivismo, (*Rivista di Filosofia e Scienze affini,* Jan.–Feb., Mar.–Apr. 1908. Reprinted in Collected Works, Vol. 10).

A. Crespi, La metafisica di H. Bergson, (*Coenobium,* July-Aug. 1908).

L. Ferri, Essai sur les données immédiates de la conscience, (*Rivista Italiana di Filosofia,* Mar.–Apr. 1890, pp. 248–9).

A. Levi, Sulle ultime forme dell' indeterminismo francese, Firenze, Civelli, 1903.

A. Levi, L'Indeterminismo nella filosofia francese contemporanea, Firenze, Seeber, 1905.

F. Masci, L'idealismo indeterminista, Napoli, 1899.

E. Morselli, Un nuovo idealismo, (H. Bergson), Udine, Tosolini, 1900.

I. Petrone, Sui limiti del determinismo scientifico, Modena, 1900 ; Roma, 1903.

G. Prezzolini, Del linguaggio come causa di errore, (H. Bergson), Firenze, Spinelli, 1904.

G. Prezzolini, La filosofia di H. Bergson, (in *La Teoria Sindacalista,* Napoli, Perrella, 1909, pp. 283–335).

F. de Sarlo, Le correnti filosofiche del secolo XIX, (*Flegrea,* III 6 ; Sept. 20, 1901, pp. 531–554).

G. Tarozzi, Della necessità nel fatto naturale ed umano, Torino, Loescher, 1896–97.

B. Varisco, La filosofia della contingenza, (*Rivista filosofica,* Vol. VIII, 1905, pp. 1–37).

B. Varisco, La Creazione, (*Rivista filosofica,* Mar.–Apr. 1908, pp. 149–180).

C. Antoniade, Filosofia lui Henri Bergson, (*Studii filosofice,* Bucarest, 1908, Vol. II, pp. 161–192 and 259–278).

F. Garcia Calderón, Dos filosofos franceses, Bergson y Boutroux, (*El Comercio,* Lima, May 5, 1907).

E. Duprat, Estudios de Filosofia contemporanea : la Filosofia de H. Bergson, (*Cultura Española,* Madrid, 1908, pp. 185–202 and 567–584).

Silberstein, L'Évolution créatrice, (Przeglad Filozoficzny, 1908).

Michal Sobeski, H. Bergson, (*Kurier Warszawski,* 20. stycznia, 1910).

AUTHOR'S PREFACE

WE necessarily express ourselves by means of words and we usually think in terms of space. That is to say, language requires us to establish between our ideas the same sharp and precise distinctions, the same discontinuity, as between material objects. This assimilation of thought to things is useful in practical life and necessary in most of the sciences. But it may be asked whether the insurmountable difficulties presented by certain philosophical problems do not arise from our placing side by side in space phenomena which do not occupy space, and whether, by merely getting rid of the clumsy symbols round which we are fighting, we might not bring the fight to an end. When an illegitimate translation of the unextended into the extended, of quality into quantity, has introduced contradiction into the very heart of the question, contradiction must, of course, recur in the answer.

The problem which I have chosen is one which is common to metaphysics and psychology, the problem of free will. | What I attempt to prove is that all discussion between the determinists and their opponents implies a previous confusion

xxiii

of duration with extensity, of succession with simultaneity, of quality with quantity: this confusion once dispelled, we may perhaps witness the disappearance of the objections raised against free will, of the definitions given of it, and, in a certain sense, of the problem of free will itself. To prove this is the object of the third part of the present volume: the first two chapters, which treat of the conceptions of intensity and duration, have been written as an introduction to the third.

H. BERGSON.

February, 1888.

CONTENTS

CHAPTER I

THE INTENSITY OF PSYCHIC STATES

CHAPTER II

THE MULTIPLICITY OF CONSCIOUS STATES
THE IDEA OF DURATION

CHAPTER III

The Organization of Conscious States
Free Will

CONCLUSION

CHAPTER I

THE INTENSITY OF PSYCHIC STATES

IT is usually admitted that states of consciousness, sensations, feelings, passions, efforts, are capable of growth and diminution ; we are even told that a sensation can be said to be twice, thrice, four times as intense as another sensation of the same kind. This latter thesis, which is maintained by psychophysicists, we shall examine later ; but even the opponents of psychophysics do not see any harm in speaking of one sensation as being more intense than another, of one effort as being greater than another, and in thus setting up differences of quantity between purely internal states. Common sense, moreover, has not the slightest hesitation in giving its verdict on this point ; people say they are more or less warm, or more or less sad, and this distinction of more and less, even when it is carried over to the region of subjective facts and unextended objects, surprises nobody. But this involves a very obscure point and a much more important problem than is usually supposed.

When we assert that one number is greater than

Can there be quantitative differences in conscious states ?

1   B

another number or one body greater than another
body, we know very well what we mean.

Such differ-
ences applica-
ble to magni-
tudes but not
to intensities. For in both cases we allude to unequal
spaces, as shall be shown in detail a
little further on, and we call that space
the greater which contains the other. But how
can a more intense sensation contain one of less
intensity ? Shall we say that the first implies the
second, that we reach the sensation of higher
intensity only on condition of having first passed
through the less intense stages of the same sensation, and that in a certain sense we are concerned,
here also, with the relation of container to contained ? This conception of intensive magnitude
seems, indeed, to be that of common sense, but we
cannot advance it as a philosophical explanation
without becoming involved in a vicious circle.
For it is beyond doubt that, in the natural series of
numbers, the later number exceeds the earlier,
but the very possibility of arranging the numbers
in ascending order arises from their having to
each other relations of container and contained,
so that we feel ourselves able to explain precisely
in what sense one is greater than the other. The
question, then, is how we succeed in forming a
series of this kind with intensities, which cannot
be superposed on each other, and by what sign
we recognize that the members of this series increase, for example, instead of diminishing : but
this always comes back to the inquiry, why an
intensity can be assimilated to a magnitude.

It is only to evade the difficulty to distinguish, as is usually done, between two species of quantity,

Alleged distinc-
tion between
two kinds of
quantity: ex-
tensive and
intensive mag-
nitude.

the first extensive and measurable, the second intensive and not admitting of measure, but of which it can neverthe-less be said that it is greater or less than another intensity. For it is recognized thereby that there is something common to these two forms of magnitude, since they are both termed magnitudes and declared to be equally capable of increase and diminution. But, from the point of view of magnitude, what can there be in common between the extensive and the intensive, the extended and the unextended? If, in the first case, we call that which contains the other the greater quantity, why go on speak-ing of quantity and magnitude when there is no longer a container or a contained? If a quantity can increase and diminish, if we perceive in it, so to speak, the *less* inside the *more*, is not such a quantity on this very account divisible, and thereby extended? Is it not then a contradiction to speak of an inex-tensive quantity? But yet common sense agrees with the philosophers in setting up a pure inten-sity as a magnitude, just as if it were something extended. And not only do we use the same word, but whether we think of a greater intensity or a greater extensity, we experience in both cases an analogous impression; the terms " greater " and " less " call up in both cases the same idea.

If we now ask ourselves in what does this idea
consist, our consciousness still offers us the image
of a container and a contained. We picture to
ourselves, for example, a greater intensity of effort
as a greater length of thread rolled up, or as a
spring which, in unwinding, will occupy a greater
space. In the idea of intensity, and even in the
word which expresses it, we shall find the image
of a present contraction and consequently a future
expansion, the image of something virtually
extended, and, if we may say so, of a compressed
space. We are thus led to believe that we
translate the intensive into the extensive, and
that we compare two intensities, or at least
express the comparison, by the confused intuition
of a relation between two extensities. But it is
just the nature of this operation which it is difficult to determine.

The solution which occurs immediately to the
mind, once it has entered upon this path, consists
in defining the intensity of a sensation,
or of any state whatever of the ego, by
the number and magnitude of the objective, and therefore measurable, causes
which have given rise to it. Doubtless,
a more intense sensation of light is the
one which has been obtained, or is
obtainable, by means of a larger number of luminous sources, provided they be at the same distance and identical with one another. But, in
the immense majority of cases, we decide about

Attempt to dis-
tinguish inten-
sities by objec-
tive causes.
But we judge of
intensity with-
out knowing
magnitude or
nature of the
cause

the intensity of the effect without even knowing the nature of the cause, much less its magnitude : indeed, it is the very intensity of the effect which often leads us to venture an hypothesis as to the number and nature of the causes, and thus to revise the judgment of our senses, which at first represented them as insignificant. And it is no use arguing that we are then comparing the actual state of the ego with some previous state in which the cause was perceived in its entirety at the same time as its effect was experienced. No doubt this is our procedure in a fairly large number of cases ; but we cannot then explain the differences of intensity which we recognize between deep-seated psychic phenomena, the cause of which is within us and not outside. On the other hand, we are never so bold in judging the intensity of a psychic state as when the subjective aspect of the phenomenon is the only one to strike us, or when the external cause to which we refer it does not easily admit of measurement. Thus it seems evident that we experience a more intense pain at the pulling out of a tooth than of a hair ; the artist knows without the possibility of doubt that the picture of a master affords him more intense pleasure than the signboard of a shop ; and there is not the slightest need ever to have heard of forces of cohesion to assert that we expend less effort in bending a steel blade than a bar of iron. Thus the comparison of two intensities is usually made without the least appreciation of the number of causes, their mode of action or their extent.

There is still room, it is true, for an hypothesis of the same nature, but more subtle. We know that mechanical, and especially kinetic, theories aim at explaining the visible and sensible properties of bodies by well defined movements of their ultimate parts, and many of us foresee the time when the intensive differences of qualities, that is to say, of our sensations, will be reduced to extensive differences between the changes taking place behind them. May it not be maintained that, without knowing these theories, we have a vague surmise of them, that behind the more intense sound we guess the presence of ampler vibrations which are propagated in the disturbed medium, and that it is with a reference to this mathematical relation, precise in itself though confusedly perceived, that we assert the higher intensity of a particular sound ? Without even going so far, could it not be laid down that every state of consciousness corresponds to a certain disturbance of the molecules and atoms of the cerebral substance, and that the intensity of a sensation measures the amplitude, the complication or the extent of these molecular movements ? This last hypothesis is at least as probable as the other, but it no more solves the problem. For, quite possibly, the intensity of a sensation bears witness to a more or

Attempt to distinguish intensities by atomic movements. But it is the sensation which is given in consciousness, and not the movement.

less considerable work accomplished in our organism ; but it is the sensation which is given to
us in consciousness, and not this mechanical work.
Indeed, it is by the intensity of the sensation
that we judge of the greater or less amount of
work accomplished : intensity then remains, at
least apparently, a property of sensation. And
still the same question recurs : why do we say
of a higher intensity that it is greater ? Why
do we think of a greater quantity or a greater
space ?

Perhaps the difficulty of the problem lies chiefly
in the fact that we call by the same name, and

**Different
kinds of in-
tensities. (1)
deep-seated
psychic states
(2) muscular
effort. Inten-
sity is more
easily defina-
ble in the for-
mer case.** picture to ourselves in the same way,
intensities which are very different in
nature, e.g. the intensity of a feeling
and that of a sensation or an effort.
The effort is accompanied by a muscular
sensation, and the sensations themselves
are connected with certain physical conditions which probably count for something in
the estimate of their intensity : we have here to
do with phenomena which take place on the surface
of consciousness, and which are always connected,
as we shall see further on, with the perception
of a movement or of an external object. But
certain states of the soul seem to us, rightly or
wrongly, to be self-sufficient, such as deep joy or
sorrow, a reflective passion or an aesthetic emotion. Pure intensity ought to be more easily

definable in these simple cases, where no extensive
element seems to be involved. We shall see, in
fact, that it is reducible here to a certain quality
or shade which spreads over a more or less considerable mass of psychic states, or, if the expression be preferred, to the larger or smaller number
of simple states which make up the fundamental
emotion.

For example, an obscure desire gradually becomes a deep passion. Now, you will see that
the feeble intensity of this desire con-

*Take, for ex-
ample, the
progress of a
desire.* sisted at first in its appearing to be
isolated and, as it were, foreign to the
remainder of your inner life. But little by little
it permeates a larger number of psychic elements,
tingeing them, so to speak, with its own colour :
and lo! your outlook on the whole of your
surroundings seems now to have changed radically. How do you become aware of a deep
passion, once it has taken hold of you, if
not by perceiving that the same objects no
longer impress you in the same manner ? All
your sensations and all your ideas seem to brighten
up : it is like childhood back again. We experience something of the kind in certain dreams, in
which we do not imagine anything out of the
ordinary, and yet through which there resounds
an indescribable note of originality. The fact is
that, the further we penetrate into the depths
of consciousness, the less right we have to treat
psychic phenomena as things which are set side

by side. When it is said that an object occupies
a large space in the soul or even that it fills it
entirely, we ought to understand by this simply
that its image has altered the shade of a thousand
perceptions or memories, and that in this sense
it pervades them, although it does not itself come
into view. But this wholly dynamic way of
looking at things is repugnant to the reflective
consciousness, because the latter delights in clean
cut distinctions, which are easily expressed in
words, and in things with well-defined outlines,
like those which are perceived in space. It will
assume then that, everything else remaining
identical, such and such a desire has gone up a
scale of magnitudes, as though it were permissible
still to speak of magnitude where there is neither
multiplicity nor space ! But just as consciousness
(as will be shown later on) concentrates on a given
point of the organism the increasing number of
muscular contractions which take place on the
surface of the body, thus converting them into
one single feeling of effort, of growing intensity,
so it will hypostatize under the form of a growing
desire the gradual alterations which take place
in the confused heap of co-existing psychic states.
But that is a change of quality rather than of
magnitude.

What makes hope such an intense pleasure
is the fact that the future, which we dispose of to
our liking, appears to us at the same time under
a multitude of forms, equally attractive and equally

possible. Even if the most coveted of these becomes realized, it will be necessary to give up the others, and we shall have lost a great deal. The idea of the future, pregnant with an infinity of possibilities, is thus more fruitful than the future itself, and this is why we find more charm in hope than in possession, in dreams than in reality.

Let us try to discover the nature of an increasing intensity of joy or sorrow in the exceptional cases where no physical symptom intervenes. Neither inner joy nor passion is an isolated inner state which at first occupies a corner of the soul and gradually spreads. At its lowest level it is very like a turning of our states of consciousness towards the future. Then, as if their weight were diminished by this attraction, our ideas and sensations succeed one another with greater rapidity ; our movements no longer cost us the same effort. Finally, in cases of extreme joy, our perceptions and memories become tinged with an indefinable quality, as with a kind of heat or light, so novel that now and then, as we stare at our own self, we wonder how it can really exist. Thus there are several characteristic forms of purely inward joy, all of which are successive stages corresponding to qualitative alterations in the whole of our psychic states. But the number of states which are concerned with each of these alterations is more or less considerable, and, without explicitly counting them, we know very

The emotions of joy and sorrow. Their successive stages correspond to qualitative changes in the whole of our psychic states.

well whether, for example, our joy pervades all
the impressions which we receive in the course of
the day or whether any escape from its influence.
We thus set up points of division in the interval
which separates two successive forms of joy, and
this gradual transition from one to the other makes
them appear in their turn as different intensities
of one and the same feeling, which is thus supposed to change in magnitude. It could be easily
shown that the different degrees of sorrow also
correspond to qualitative changes. Sorrow begins
by being nothing more than a facing towards the
past, an impoverishment of our sensations and
ideas, as if each of them were now contained
entirely in the little which it gives out, as if the
future were in some way stopped up. And it
ends with an impression of crushing failure, the
effect of which is that we aspire to nothingness,
while every new misfortune, by making us understand better the uselessness of the struggle,
causes us a bitter pleasure.

The aesthetic feelings offer us a still more
striking example of this progressive stepping in
of new elements, which can be detected
in the fundamental emotion and which
seem to increase its magnitude, although
in reality they do nothing more than
alter its nature. Let us consider the simplest
of them, the feeling of grace. At first it is only
the perception of a certain ease, a certain facility
in the outward movements. And as those move-

The aesthetic feelings. Their increasing in-tensities are really differ-ent feelings.

ments are easy which prepare the way for others,
we are led to find a superior ease in the movements
which can be foreseen, in the present attitudes
in which future attitudes are pointed out and, as
it were, prefigured. If jerky movements are
wanting in grace, the reason is that each of them
is self-sufficient and does not announce those
which are to follow. If curves are more graceful
than broken lines, the reason is that, while a curved
line changes its direction at every moment, every
new direction is indicated in the preceding one.
Thus the perception of ease in motion passes over
into the pleasure of mastering the flow of time
and of holding the future in the present. A third
element comes in when the graceful movements
submit to a rhythm and are accompanied by music.
For the rhythm and measure, by allowing us to foresee to a still greater extent the movements of the
dancer, make us believe that we now control them.
As we guess almost the exact attitude which
the dancer is going to take, he seems to obey us
when he really takes it : the regularity of the
rhythm establishes a kind of communication between him and us, and the periodic returns of the
measure are like so many invisible threads by
means of which we set in motion this imaginary
puppet. Indeed, if it stops for an instant, our
hand in its impatience cannot refrain from making
a movement, as though to push it, as though to
replace it in the midst of this movement, the
rhythm of which has taken complete possession

of our thought and will. Thus a kind of physical sympathy enters into the feeling of grace. Now, in analysing the charm of this sympathy, you will find that it pleases you through its affinity with moral sympathy, the idea of which it subtly suggests. This last element, in which the others are merged after having in a measure ushered it in, explains the irresistible attractiveness of grace. We could hardly make out why it affords us such pleasure if it were nothing but a saving of effort, as Spencer maintains.[1] But the truth is that in anything which we call very graceful we imagine ourselves able to detect, besides the lightness which is a sign of mobility, some suggestion of a possible movement towards ourselves, of a virtual and even nascent sympathy. It is this mobile sympathy, always ready to offer itself, which is just the essence of higher grace. Thus the increasing intensities of aesthetic feeling are here resolved into as many different feelings, each one of which, already heralded by its predecessor, becomes perceptible in it and then completely eclipses it. It is this qualitative progress which we interpret as a change of magnitude, because we like simple thoughts and because our language is ill-suited to render the subtleties of psychological analysis.

To understand how the feeling of the beautiful itself admits of degrees, we should have to submit

---

[1] *Essays*, (Library Edition, 1891), Vol. ii, p. 381.

it to a minute analysis. Perhaps the difficulty

which we experience in defining it is
largely owing to the fact that we look
upon the beauties of nature as an-
terior to those of art : the processes
of art are thus supposed to be nothing
more than means by which the artist expresses
the beautiful, and the essence of the beautiful
remains unexplained. But we might ask ourselves whether nature is beautiful otherwise than
through meeting by chance certain processes of
our art, and whether, in a certain sense, art is not
prior to nature. Without even going so far, it
seems more in conformity with the rules of a sound
method to study the beautiful first in the works
in which it has been produced by a conscious effort,
and then to pass on by imperceptible steps from
art to nature, which may be looked upon as an
artist in its own way. By placing ourselves at this
point of view, we shall perceive that the object of
art is to put to sleep the active or rather resistant
powers of our personality, and thus to bring us
into a state of perfect responsiveness, in which
we realize the idea that is suggested to us and sympathize with the feeling that is expressed. In the
processes of art we shall find, in a weakened form, a
refined and in some measure spiritualized version
of the processes commonly used to induce the state
of hypnosis. Thus, in music, the rhythm and
measure suspend the normal flow of our sensations
and ideas by causing our attention to swing to and

fro between fixed points, and they take hold of us
with such force that even the faintest imitation
of a groan will suffice to fill us with the utmost
sadness.   If musical sounds affect us more power-
fully than the sounds of nature, the reason is that
nature confines itself to *expressing* feelings, whereas music *suggests* them to us.   Whence indeed
comes the charm of poetry ?   The poet is he with
whom feelings develop into images, and the images
themselves into words which translate them while
obeying the laws of rhythm.   In seeing these
images pass before our eyes we in our turn experience the feeling which was, so to speak, their
emotional equivalent : but we should never realize
these images so strongly without the regular movements of the rhythm by which our soul is lulled
into self-forgetfulness, and, as in a dream, thinks
and sees with the poet.   The plastic arts obtain
an effect of the same kind by the fixity which
they suddenly impose upon life, and which a
physical contagion carries over to the attention of
the spectator.   While the works of ancient sculpture express faint emotions which play upon them
like a passing breath, the pale immobility of the
stone causes the feeling expressed or the movement just begun to appear as if they were fixed for
ever, absorbing our thought and our will in their
own eternity.   We find in architecture, in the
very midst of this startling immobility, certain
effects analogous to those of rhythm.   The sym-
metry of form, the indefinite repetition of the same

architectural motive, causes our faculty of perception to oscillate between the same and the same again, and gets rid of those customary incessant changes which in ordinary life bring us back without ceasing to the consciousness of our personality : even the faint suggestion of an idea will then be enough to make the idea fill the whole of our mind. Thus art aims at impressing feelings on us rather than expressing them ; it suggests them to us, and willingly dispenses with the imitation of nature when it finds some more efficacious means. Nature, like art, proceeds by suggestion, but does not command the resources of rhythm. It supplies the deficiency by the long comradeship, based on influences received in common by nature and by ourselves, of which the effect is that the slightest indication by nature of a feeling arouses sympathy in our minds, just as a mere gesture on the part of the hypnotist is enough to force the intended suggestion upon a subject accustomed to his control. And this sympathy is shown in particular when nature displays to us beings of *normal* proportions, so that our attention is distributed equally over all the parts of the figure without being fixed on any one of them : our perceptive faculty then finds itself lulled and soothed by this harmony, and nothing hinders any longer the free play of sympathy, which is ever ready to come forward as soon as the obstacle in its path is removed.

It follows from this analysis that the feeling of

the beautiful is no specific feeling, but that every feeling experienced by us will assume an aesthetic character, provided that it has been *suggested*, and not *caused*. It will now be understood why the aesthetic emotion seems to us to admit of degrees of intensity, and also of degrees of elevation. Sometimes the feeling which is suggested scarcely makes a break in the compact texture of psychic phenomena of which our history consists ; sometimes it draws our attention from them, but not so that they become lost to sight ; sometimes, finally, it puts itself in their place, engrosses us and completely monopolizes our soul. There are thus distinct phases in the progress of an aesthetic feeling, as in the state of hypnosis ; and these phases correspond less to variations of degree than to differences of state or of nature. But the merit of a work of art is not measured so much by the power with which the suggested feeling takes hold of us as by the richness of this feeling itself : in other words, besides degrees of intensity we instinctively distinguish degrees of depth or elevation. If this last concept be analysed, it will be seen that the feelings and thoughts which the artist suggests to us express and sum up a more or less considerable part of his history. If the art which gives only sensations is an inferior art, the reason is that analysis often fails to discover in a sensation anything beyond the sensation itself. But the greater number of emotions are instinct with a

c

thousand sensations, feelings or ideas which pervade them : each one is then a state unique of its kind and indefinable, and it seems that we should have to re-live the life of the subject who experiences it if we wished to grasp it in its original complexity. Yet the artist aims at giving us a share in this emotion, so rich, so personal, so novel, and at enabling us to experience what he cannot make us understand. This he will bring about by choosing, among the outward signs of his emotions, those which our body is likely to imitate mechanically, though slightly, as soon as it perceives them, so as to transport us all at once into the indefinable psychological state which called them forth. Thus will be broken down the barrier interposed by time and space between his consciousness and ours : and the richer in ideas and the more pregnant with sensations and emotions is the feeling within whose limits the artist has brought us, the deeper and the higher shall we find the beauty thus expressed. The successive intensities of the æsthetic feeling thus correspond to changes of state occurring in us, and the degrees of depth to the larger or smaller number of elementary psychic phenomena which we dimly discern in the fundamental emotion.

The moral feelings might be studied in the same way. Let us take pity as an example. It consists in the first place in putting oneself mentally in the place of others, in suffering their pain. But if it were

The moral feelings. Pity. Its increasing intensity is a qualitative progress.

nothing more, as some have maintained, it would
inspire us with the idea of avoiding the wretched
rather than helping them, for pain is naturally
abhorrent to us.   This feeling of horror may indeed
be at the root of pity ; but a new element soon
comes in, the need of helping our fellow-men and of
alleviating their suffering.   Shall we say with La
Rochefoucauld that this so-called sympathy is a
calculation, " a shrewd insurance against evils to
come " ?   Perhaps a dread of some future evil
to ourselves does hold a place in our compassion
for other people's evil.   These however are but
lower forms of pity.   True pity consists not so
much in fearing suffering as in desiring it.   The
desire is a faint one and we should hardly wish to
see it realized ; yet we form it in spite of ourselves,
as if Nature were committing some great injustice
and it were necessary to get rid of all suspicion
of complicity with her.   The essence of pity is thus
a need for self-abasement, an aspiration down-
wards.   This painful aspiration nevertheless has a
charm about it, because it raises us in our own
estimation and makes us feel superior to those
sensuous goods from which our thought is tem-
porarily detached.   The increasing intensity of
pity thus consists in a qualitative progress, in a
transition from repugnance to fear, from fear
to sympathy, and from sympathy itself to hu-
mility.

We do not propose to carry this analysis any further. The psychic states whose intensity we have just defined are deep-seated states which

Conscious states connected with external causes or involving physical symptoms.

do not seem to have any close relation to their external cause or to involve the perception of muscular contraction. But such states are rare. There is hardly any passion or desire, any joy or sorrow, which is not accompanied by physical symptoms ; and, where these symptoms occur, they probably count for something in the estimate of intensities. As for the sensations properly so called, they are manifestly connected with their external cause, and though the intensity of the sensation cannot be defined by the magnitude of its cause, there undoubtedly exists some relation between these two terms. In some of its manifestations consciousness even appears to spread outwards, as if intensity were being developed into extensity, e.g. in the case of muscular effort. Let us face this last phenomenon at once : we shall thus be transported at a bound to the opposite extremity of the series of psychic phenomena.

If there is a phenomenon which seems to be presented immediately to consciousness under the

Muscular effort seems at first sight to be quantitative.

form of quantity or at least of magnitude, it is undoubtedly muscular effort. We picture to our minds a psychic force imprisoned in the soul like the winds in the cave of Aeolus, and only waiting for an opportunity to burst forth : our will is supposed to watch over this force and from time to time to open a passage for it, regulating the outflow by the effect which it is desired to produce. If we consider the matter carefully, we shall see that this somewhat crude conception of effort plays a large part in our belief in intensive magnitudes. Muscular force, whose sphere of action is space and which manifests itself in phenomena admitting of measure, seems to us to have existed previous to its manifestations, but in smaller volume, and, so to speak, in a compressed state : hence we do not hesitate to reduce this volume more and more, and finally we believe that we can understand how a purely psychic state, which does not occupy space, can nevertheless possess magnitude. Science, too, tends to strengthen the illusion of common sense with regard to this point. Bain, for example, declares that " the sensibility accompanying muscular movement coincides with the *outgoing* stream of nervous energy : "[1] it is thus just the emission of nervous force which consciousness perceives. Wundt also speaks of a sensation, central in its origin, accompanying the voluntary innervation of the muscles, and quotes the example of the paralytic " who has a very distinct sensation of the force which he employs in the effort to raise his leg, although it remains motionless." [2] Most of the

---

[1] *The Senses and the Intellect*, 4th ed., (1894), p. 79.

[2] *Grundzüge der Physiologischen Psychologie*, 2nd ed. (1880), Vol. i, p. 375

authorities adhere to this opinion, which would be the unanimous view of positive science were it not that several years ago Professor William James drew the attention of physiologists to certain phenomena which had been but little remarked, although they were very remarkable.

When a paralytic strives to raise his useless limb, he certainly does not execute this movement, but, with or without his will, he executes another. Some movement is carried out somewhere : otherwise there is no sensation of effort.[1] Vulpian had already called attention to the fact that if a man affected with hemiplegia is told to clench his paralysed fist, he unconsciously carries out this action with the fist which is not affected. Ferrier described a still more curious phenomenon.[2] Stretch out your arm while slightly bending your forefinger, as if you were going to press the trigger of a pistol ; without moving the finger, without contracting any muscle of the hand, without producing any apparent movement, you will yet be able to feel that you are expending energy. On a closer examination, however, you will perceive that this sensation of effort coincides

The feeling of effort. We are conscious not of an expenditure of force but of the resulting muscular movement.

---

[1] W. James, *Le sentiment de l'effort* (*Critique philosophique*, 1880, Vol. ii,) [cf. *Principles of Psychology*, (1891), Vol. ii, chap. xxvi.]

[2] *Functions of the Brain*, 2nd ed. (1886), p. 386.

with the fixation of the muscles of your chest, that you keep your glottis closed and actively contract your respiratory muscles. As soon as respiration resumes its normal course the consciousness of effort vanishes, unless you really move your finger. These facts already seemed to show that we are conscious, not of an expenditure of force, but of the movement of the muscles which results from it. The new feature in Professor James's investigation is that he has verified the hypothesis in the case of examples which seemed to contradict it absolutely. Thus when the external rectus muscle of the right eye is paralysed, the patient tries in vain to turn his eye towards the right ; yet objects seem to him to recede towards the right, and since the act of volition has produced no effect, it follows, said Helmholtz,[1] that he is conscious of the effort of volition. But, replies Professor James, no account has been taken of what goes on in the other eye. This remains covered during the experiments ; nevertheless it moves and there is not much trouble in proving that it does. It is the movement of the left eye, perceived by consciousness, which produces the sensation of effort together with the impression that the objects perceived by the right eye are moving. These and similar observations lead Professor James to assert that the feeling

---

[1] *Handbuch der Physiologischen Optik*, 1st ed. (1867), pp. 600-601.

of effort is centripetal and not centrifugal. We are not conscious of a force which we are supposed to launch upon our organism : our feeling of muscular energy at work " is a complex afferent sensation, which comes from contracted muscles, stretched ligaments, compressed joints, an immobilized chest, a closed glottis, a knit brow, clenched jaws," in a word, from all the points of the periphery where the effort causes an alteration.

It is not for us to take a side in the dispute. After all, the question with which we have to deal is not whether the feeling of effort comes from the centre or the periphery, but in what does our perception of its intensity exactly consist ? Now, it is sufficient to observe oneself attentively to reach a conclusion on this point which Professor James has not formulated, but which seems to us quite in accord with the spirit of his teaching. We maintain that the more a given effort seems to us to increase, the greater is the number of muscles which contract in sympathy with it, and that the apparent consciousness of a greater intensity of effort at a given point of the organism is reducible, in reality, to the perception of a larger surface of the body being affected.

Try, for example, to clench the fist with increasing force. You will have the impression of a sensation of effort entirely localized in your hand and running up a scale of magnitudes. In reality, what you experience in your hand

Intensity of feeling of effort proportional to extent of our body affected.

remains the same, but the sensation which was
at first localized there has affected

Our con-
sciousness of
an increase of
muscular ef-
fort consists in
the perception
of (1) a great-
er number of
peripheral
sensations (2)
a qualitative
change in
some of them. your arm and ascended to the shoulder ;
finally, the other arm stiffens, both legs
do the same, the respiration is checked ;
it is the whole body which is at work.
But you fail to notice distinctly all these
concomitant movements unless you are
warned of them : till then you thought
you were dealing with a single state of consciousness
which changed in magnitude. When you press
your lips more and more tightly against one another,
you believe that you are experiencing in your lips
one and the same sensation which is continually
increasing in strength : here again further reflection will show you that this sensation remains
identical, but that certain muscles of the face and
the head and then of all the rest of the body have
taken part in the operation. You felt this gradual
encroachment, this increase of the surface affected,
which is in truth a change of quantity ; but, as
your attention was concentrated on your closed
lips, you localized the increase there and you
made the psychic force there expended into a
magnitude, although it possessed no extensity.
Examine carefully somebody who is lifting heavier
and heavier weights : the muscular contraction
gradually spreads over his whole body. As for
the special sensation which he experiences in the
arm which is at work, it remains constant for a
very long time and hardly changes except in

quality, the weight becoming at a certain moment fatigue, and the fatigue pain. Yet the subject will imagine that he is conscious of a continual increase in the psychic force flowing into his arm. He will not recognize his mistake unless he is warned of it, so inclined is he to measure a given psychic state by the conscious movements which accompany it ! From these facts and from many others of the same kind we believe we can deduce the following conclusion : our consciousness of an increase of muscular effort is reducible to the twofold perception of a greater number of peripheral sensations, and of a qualitative change occurring in some of them.

We are thus led to define the intensity of a superficial effort in the same way as that of a deep-seated psychic feeling. In both

The same definition of intensity applies to superficial efforts, deep-seated feelings and states intermediate between the two.

cases there is a qualitative progress and an increasing complexity, indistinctly perceived. But consciousness, accustomed to think in terms of space and to translate its thoughts into words, will denote the feeling by a single word and will localize the effort at the exact point where it yields a useful result : it will then become aware of an effort which is always of the same nature and increases at the spot assigned to it, and a feeling which, retaining the same name, grows without changing its nature. Now, the same illusion of consciousness is likely to be met with again in the case of the states which are inter-

mediate between superficial efforts and deep-
seated feelings.   A large number of psychic states
are accompanied, in fact, by muscular contractions
and peripheral sensations.   Sometimes these superficial elements are co-ordinated by a purely specu-
lative idea, sometimes by an idea of a practical
order.   In the first case there is intellectual effort
or attention ; in the second we have the emotions
which may be called violent or acute : anger, terror,
and certain varieties of joy, sorrow, passion and
desire.   Let us show briefly that the same definition of intensity applies to these intermediate
states.

Attention is not a purely physiological phenomenon, but we cannot deny that it is accompanied
by movements.   These movements are
neither the cause nor the result of the
phenomenon ; they are part of it, they
express it in terms of space, as Ribot
has so remarkably proved.[1]   Fechner had already
reduced the effort of attention in a sense-organ to
the muscular feeling " produced by putting in
motion, by a sort of reflex action, the muscles
which are correlated with the different sense
organs."   He had noticed the very distinct sensation of tension and contraction of the scalp, the
pressure from without inwards over the whole
skull, which we experience when we make a great
effort to recall something.   Ribot has studied

The interme-
diate states.
Attention and
its relation to
muscular con-
traction.

[1] *Le mécanisme de l'attention.*   Alcan, 1888.

more closely the movements which are characteristic of voluntary attention. " Attention con-
tracts the frontal muscle : this muscle . . .
draws the eyebrow towards itself, raises it and
causes transverse wrinkles on the forehead. . . .
In extreme cases the mouth is opened wide. With
children and with many adults eager attention gives
rise to a protrusion of the lips, a kind of pout."
Certainly, a purely psychic factor will always
enter into voluntary attention, even if it be
nothing more than the exclusion by the will of all
ideas foreign to the one with which the subject
wishes to occupy himself. But, once this exclusion
is made, we believe that we are still conscious of a
growing tension of soul, of an immaterial effort
which increases. Analyse this impression and
you will find nothing but the feeling of a muscular
contraction which spreads over a wider surface or
changes its nature, so that the tension becomes
pressure, fatigue and pain.

Now, we do not see any essential difference
between the effort of attention and what may be
The intensity called the effort of psychic tension :
of violent emo-
tions as mus- acute desire, uncontrolled anger, passion-
cular tension. ate love, violent hatred. Each of these
states may be reduced, we believe, to a system of
muscular contractions co-ordinated by an idea ; but
in the case of attention, it is the more or less reflective idea of knowing ; in the case of emotion, the
unreflective idea of acting. The intensity of these
violent emotions is thus likely to be nothing but

the muscular tension which accompanies them. Darwin has given a remarkable description of the physiological symptoms of rage. " The action of the heart is much accelerated. . . . The face reddens or may turn deadly pale. The respiration is laboured, the chest heaves, and the dilated nostrils quiver. The whole body often trembles. The voice is affected. The teeth are clenched or ground together and the muscular system is commonly stimulated to violent, almost frantic action. The gestures . . . represent more or less plainly the act of striking or fighting with an enemy." [1] We shall not go so far as to maintain, with Professor James, [2] that the emotion of rage is reducible to the sum of these organic sensations : there will always be an irreducible psychic element in anger, if this be only the idea of striking or fighting, of which Darwin speaks, and which gives a common direction to so many diverse movements. But, though this idea determines the direction of the emotional state and the accompanying movements, the growing intensity of the state itself is, we believe, nothing but the deeper and deeper disturbance of the organism, a disturbance which consciousness has no difficulty in measuring by the number and extent of the bodily surfaces concerned. It will be useless to assert that there is a restrained rage which is all the more intense. The reason is that, where emotion has free play, consciousness does not

[1] *The Expression of the Emotions.* 1st ed., (1872), p. 74.
[2] " What is an Emotion ? " *Mind*, 1884, p. 189.

dwell on the details of the accompanying movements, but it does dwell upon them and is concentrated upon them when its object is to conceal them.
Eliminate, in short, all trace of organic disturbance,
all tendency towards muscular contraction, and
all that will be left of anger will be the idea, or, if
you still insist on making it an emotion, you will
be unable to assign it any intensity.

"Fear, when strong," says Herbert Spencer,
"expresses itself in cries, in efforts to escape, in
palpitations, in tremblings."[1] We go
Intensity and reflex movements. No essential difference between intensity of deep-seated feelings and that of violent emotions. further, and maintain that these movements form part of the terror itself : by
their means the terror becomes an
emotion capable of passing through
different degrees of intensity. Suppress
them entirely, and the more or less
intense state of terror will be succeeded by an
idea of terror, the wholly intellectual representation
of a danger which it concerns us to avoid. There
are also high degrees of joy and sorrow, of desire,
aversion and even shame, the height of which will
be found to be nothing but the reflex movements
begun by the organism and perceived by consciousness. "When lovers meet," says Darwin, "we
know that their hearts beat quickly, their breathing
is hurried and their faces flushed."[2] Aversion
is marked by movements of repugnance which we
repeat without noticing when we think of the

[1] *Principles of Psychology*, 3rd. ed., (1890), Vol. i, p. 482.
[2] *The Expression of the Emotions*. 1st ed., p. 78.

object of our dislike. We blush and involuntarily clench the fingers when we feel shame, even if it be retrospective. The acuteness of these emotions is estimated by the number and nature of the peripheral sensations which accompany them. Little by little, and in proportion as the emotional state loses its violence and gains in depth, the peripheral sensations will give place to inner states ; it will be no longer our outward movements but our ideas, our memories, our states of consciousness of every description, which will turn in larger or smaller numbers in a definite direction. There is, then, no essential difference from the point of view of intensity between the deep-seated feelings, of which we spoke at the beginning, and the acute or violent emotions which we have just passed in review. To say that love, hatred, desire, increase in violence is to assert that they are projected outwards, that they radiate to the surface, that peripheral sensations are substituted for inner states : but superficial or deep-seated, violent or reflective, the intensity of these feelings always consists in the multiplicity of simple states which consciousness dimly discerns in them.

We have hitherto confined ourselves to feelings and efforts, complex states the intensity of which **Magnitude of** does not absolutely depend on an ex-**sensations.** **Affective and** ternal cause. But sensations seem to us **representative** **sensations.** ʾimple states: in what will their magnitude

consist ?   The intensity of sensations varies with
the external cause of which they are said to be
the conscious equivalent : how shall we explain the
presence of quantity in an effect which is inextensive, and in this case indivisible?   To answer this
question, we must first distinguish between the
so-called affective and the representative sensations.   There is no doubt that we pass gradually
from the one to the other and that some affective
element enters into the majority of our simple
representations.   But nothing prevents us from
isolating this element and inquiring separately,
in what does the intensity of an affective sensation,
a pleasure or a pain, consist ?

Perhaps the difficulty of the latter problem is principally due to the fact that we are unwilling to see
Affective sen- in the affective state anything but the
sations and   conscious expression of an organic disturb-
organic dis-
turbance.   ance, the inward echo of an outward cause.
We notice that a more intense sensation generally
corresponds to a greater nervous disturbance ;
but inasmuch as these disturbances are unconscious as movements, since they come before consciousness in the guise of a sensation which has
no resemblance at all to motion, we do not see
how they could transmit to the sensation anything
of their own magnitude.   For there is nothing
in common, we repeat, between superposable
magnitudes such as, for example, vibration-
amplitudes, and sensations which do not occupy

space. If the more intense sensation seems to us to contain the less intense, if it assumes for us, like the physical impression itself, the form of a magnitude, the reason probably is that it retains something of the physical impression to which it corresponds. And it will retain nothing of it if it is merely the conscious translation of a movement of molecules ; for, just because this movement is translated into the sensation of pleasure or pain, it remains unconscious as molecular movement.

But it might be asked whether pleasure and pain, instead of expressing only what has just occurred, or what is actually occurring, in the organism, as is usually believed, could not also point out what is going to, or what is tending to take place. It seems indeed somewhat improbable that nature, so profoundly utilitarian, should have here assigned to consciousness the merely scientific task of informing us about the past or the present, which no longer depend upon us. It must be noticed in addition that we rise by imperceptible stages from automatic to free movements, and that the latter differ from the former principally in introducing an affective sensation between the external action which occasions them and the volitional reaction which ensues. Indeed, all our actions might have been automatic, and we can surmise that there are many organized beings in whose case an external stimulus causes a definite reaction without calling up consciousness as an

Pleasure and pain as signs of the future reaction rather than psychic translations of the past stimulus.

D

intermediate agent. If pleasure and pain make their appearance in certain privileged beings, it is probably to call forth a resistance to the automatic reaction which would have taken place: either sensation has nothing to do, or it is nascent freedom. But how would it enable us to resist the reaction which is in preparation if it did not acquaint us with the nature of the latter by some definite sign? And what can this sign be except the sketching, and, as it were, the prefiguring of the future automatic movements in the very midst of the sensation which is being experienced? The affective state must then correspond not merely to the physical disturbances, movements or phenomena which have taken place, but also, and especially, to those which are in preparation, those which are getting ready to be.

It is certainly not obvious at first sight how this hypothesis simplifies the problem. For we are

Intensity of affective sensations would then be our consciousness of the involuntary movements tending to follow the stimulus.
trying to find what there can be in common, from the point of view of magnitude, between a physical phenomenon and a state of consciousness, and we seem to have merely turned the difficulty round by making the present state of consciousness a sign of the future reaction, rather than a psychic translation of the past stimulus. But the difference between the two hypotheses is considerable. For the molecular disturbances which were mentioned just now are necessarily unconscious, since no trace of the movements

themselves can be actually perceived in the
sensation which translates them. But the automatic movements which tend to follow the stimulus
as its natural outcome are likely to be conscious
as movements : or else the sensation itself, whose
function is to invite us to choose between this
automatic reaction and other possible movements,
would be of no avail. The intensity of affective
sensations might thus be nothing more than our
consciousness of the involuntary movements which
are being begun and outlined, so to speak, within
these states, and which would have gone on in
their own way if nature had made us automata
instead of conscious beings.

If such be the case, we shall not compare a pain
of increasing intensity to a note which grows
louder and louder, but rather to a
symphony, in which an increasing number of instruments make themselves
heard. Within the characteristic sensation, which gives the tone to all the others,
consciousness distinguishes a larger or smaller
number of sensations arising at different points
of the periphery, muscular contractions, organic
movements of every kind : the choir of these
elementary psychic states voices the new demands
of the organism, when confronted by a new situation. In other words, we estimate the intensity
of a pain by the larger or smaller part of the
organism which takes interest in it. Richet [1]

Intensity of a pain estimated by extent of organism affected.

[1] *L'homme et l'intelligence*, p. 36.

has observed that the slighter the pain, the more precisely is it referred to a particular spot ; if it becomes more intense, it is referred to the whole of the member affected. And he concludes by saying that " the pain spreads in proportion as it is more intense." [1] We should rather reverse the sentence, and define the intensity of the pain by the very number and extent of the parts of the body which sympathize with it and react, and whose reactions are perceived by consciousness. To convince ourselves of this, it will be enough to read the remarkable description of disgust given by the same author : " If the stimulus is slight there may be neither nausea nor vomiting. . . . If the stimulus is stronger, instead of being confined to the pneumo-gastric nerve, it spreads and affects almost the whole organic system. The face turns pale, the smooth muscles of the skin contract, the skin is covered with a cold perspiration, the heart stops beating : in a word there is a general organic disturbance following the stimulation of the medulla oblongata, and this disturbance is the supreme expression of disgust." [2] But is it nothing more than its expression ? In what will the general sensation of disgust consist, if not in the sum of these elementary sensations ? And what can we understand here by increasing intensity, if it is not the constantly increasing number of sensations

---

[1] Ibid. p. 37.   [2] Ibid. p. 43.

which join in with the sensations already experienced ? Darwin has drawn a striking picture of the reactions following a pain which becomes more and more acute. " Great pain urges all animals . . . to make the most violent and diversified efforts to escape from the cause of suffering. . . . With men the mouth may be closely compressed, or more commonly the lips are retracted with the teeth clenched or ground together. . . . The eyes stare wildly . . . or the brows are heavily contracted. Perspiration bathes the body. . . . The circulation and respiration are much affected." [1] Now, is it not by this very contraction of the muscles affected that we measure the intensity of a pain ? Analyse your idea of any suffering which you call extreme : do you not mean that it is unbearable, that is to say, that it urges the organism to a thousand different actions in order to escape from it ? I can picture to myself a nerve transmitting a pain which is independent of all automatic reaction ; and I can equally understand that stronger or weaker stimulations influence this nerve differently. But I do not see how these differences of sensation would be interpreted by our consciousness as differences of quantity unless we connected them with the reactions which usually accompany them, and which are more or less extended and more or

[1] *The Expression of the Emotions.* 1st ed., pp. 72, 69, 70.

less important. Without these subsequent reactions, the intensity of the pain would be a
quality, and not a magnitude.

We have hardly any other means of comparing
several pleasures with one another. What do
Pleasures com- we mean by a greater pleasure except a
pared by bod-
ily inclination. pleasure that is preferred? And what
                can our preference be, except a certain
disposition of our organs, the effect of which
is that, when two pleasures are offered simultaneously to our mind, our body inclines towards one
of them? Analyse this inclination itself and
you will find a great many little movements which
begin and become perceptible in the organs concerned, and even in the rest of the body, as if the
organism were coming forth to meet the pleasure
as soon as it is pictured. When we define inclination as a movement, we are not using a metaphor.
When confronted by several pleasures pictured
by our mind, our body turns towards one of them
spontaneously, as though by a reflex action.
It rests with us to check it, but the attraction
of the pleasure is nothing but this movement
that is begun, and the very keenness of the pleasure, while we enjoy it, is merely the inertia
of the organism, which is immersed in it and
rejects every other sensation. Without this *vis
inertiae* of which we become conscious by the
very resistance which we offer to anything that
might distract us, pleasure would be a state,
but no longer a magnitude. In the moral as in

the physical world, attraction serves to define movement rather than to produce it.

We have studied the affective sensations separately, but we must now notice that many representative sensations possess an affective character, and thus call forth a reaction on our part which we take into account in estimating their intensity. A considerable increase of light is represented for us by a characteristic sensation which is not yet pain, but which is analogous to dazzling. In proportion as the amplitude of sound-vibrations increases, our head and then our body seem to us to vibrate or to receive a shock. Certain representative sensations, those of taste, smell and temperature, have a fixed character of pleasantness or unpleasantness. Between flavours which are more or less bitter you will hardly distinguish anything but differences of quality; they are like different shades of one and the same colour. But these differences of quality are at once interpreted as differences of quantity, because of their affective character and the more or less pronounced movements of reaction, pleasure or repugnance, which they suggest to us. Besides, even when the sensation remains purely representative, its external cause cannot exceed a certain degree of strength or weakness without inciting us to movements which enable us to measure it. Sometimes indeed

The intensity of representative sensations. Many also affective and intensity is measured by reaction called forth. In others a new element enters.

we have to make an effort to perceive this sensation, as if it were trying to escape notice ; sometimes on the other hand it obsesses us, forces
itself upon us and engrosses us to such an extent
that we make every effort to escape from it and
to remain ourselves. In the former case the
sensation is said to be of slight intensity, and in
the latter case very intense. Thus, in order to
perceive a distant sound, to distinguish what
we call a faint smell or a dim light, we strain all
our faculties, we " pay attention." And it is
just because the smell and the light thus require
to be reinforced by our efforts that they seem
to us feeble. And, inversely, we recognize a
sensation of extreme intensity by the irresistible
reflex movements to which it incites us, or by
the powerlessness with which it affects us. When
a cannon is fired off close to our ears or a dazzling
light suddenly flares up, we lose for an instant
the consciousness of our personality ; this state
may even last some time in the case of a very
nervous subject. It must be added that, even
within the range of the so-called medium intensities, when we are dealing on even terms with a
representative sensation, we often estimate its
importance by comparing it with another which
it drives away, or by taking account of the per-
sistence with which it returns. Thus the ticking
of a watch seems louder at night because it easily
monopolizes a consciousness almost empty of
sensations and ideas. Foreigners talking to one

another in a language which we do not understand seem to us to speak very loudly, because
their words no longer call up any ideas in our
mind, and thus break in upon a kind of intellectual
silence and monopolize our attention like the
ticking of a watch at night. With these so-called
medium sensations, however, we approach a
series of psychic states, the intensity of which
is likely to possess a new meaning. For, in
most cases, the organism hardly reacts at all, at
least in a way that can be perceived ; and yet
we still make a magnitude out of the pitch of
a sound, the intensity of a light, the saturation
of a colour. Doubtless, a closer observation of
what takes place in the whole of the organism
when we hear such and such a note or perceive
such and such a colour has more than one surprise in store for us. Has not C. Féré shown
that every sensation is accompanied by an increase in muscular force which can be measured
by the dynamometer ?[1] But of an increase of this
kind there is hardly any consciousness at all,
and if we reflect on the precision with which we
distinguish sounds and colours, nay, even weights
and temperatures, we shall easily guess that
some new element must come into play in our
estimate of them.

Now, the nature of this element is easy to deter-

[1] C. Féré, *Sensation et Mouvement*. Paris, 1887.

mine. For, in proportion as a sensation loses its affective character and becomes representative, the reactions which it called forth on our part tend to disappear, but at the same time we perceive the external object which is its cause, or if we do not now perceive it, we have perceived it, and we think of it. Now, this cause is extensive and therefore measurable : a constant experience, which began with the first glimmerings of consciousness and which continues throughout the whole of our life, shows us a definite shade of sensation corresponding to a definite amount of stimulation. We thus associate the idea of a certain quantity of cause with a certain quality of effect ; and finally, as happens in the case of every acquired perception, we transfer the idea into the sensation, the quantity of the cause into the quality of the effect. At this very moment the intensity, which was nothing but a certain shade or quality of the sensation, becomes a magnitude. We shall easily understand this process if, for example, we hold a pin in our right hand and prick our left hand more and more deeply. At first we shall feel as it were a tickling, then a touch which is succeeded by a prick, then a pain localized at a point, and finally the spreading of this pain over the surrounding zone. And the more we reflect on it, the more clearly shall we see that we are here dealing with so many qualitatively distinct sensations,

The purely representative sensations are measured by their external causes.

so many varieties of a single species. But yet
we spoke at first of one and the same sensation
which spread further and further, of one prick
which increased in intensity. The reason is that,
without noticing it, we localized in the sensation
of the left hand, which is pricked, the progressive
effort of the right hand, which pricks. We thus
introduced the caus? into the effect, and unconsciously interpreted quality as quantity, intensity as magnitude. Now, it is easy to see that
the intensity of every representative sensation
ought to be understood in the same way.

The sensations of sound display well marked
degrees of intensity. We have already spoken
of the necessity of taking into account
the affective character of these sensations, the shock received by the whole
of the organism. We have shown that
a very intense sound is one which engrosses our attention, which supplants all the
others. But take away the shock, the well-
marked vibration, which you sometimes feel
in your head or even throughout your body :
take away the clash which takes place between
sounds heard simultaneously : what will be left
except an indefinable quality of the sound which
is heard ? But this quality is immediately interpreted as quantity because you have obtained
it yourself a thousand times, e.g. by striking
some object and thus expending a definite quantity of effort. You know, too, how far you would

The sensa-
tions of sound.
Intensity mea-
sured by effort
necessary to
produce a sim-
ilar sound.

have to raise your voice to produce a similar
sound, and the idea of this effort immediately
comes into your mind when you transform the
intensity of the sound into a magnitude.   Wundt [1]
has drawn attention to the quite special connexions of vocal and auditory nervous filaments
which are met with in the human brain.   And has
it not been said that to hear is to speak to oneself ?   Some neuropaths cannot be present at
a conversation without moving their lips ;   this
is only an exaggeration of what takes place in
the case of every one of us.   How will the ex-
pressive or rather suggestive power of music be
explained, if not by admitting that we repeat
to ourselves the sounds heard, so as to carry
ourselves back into the psychic state out of which
they emerged, an original state, which nothing
will express, but which something may suggest,
viz., the very motion and attitude which the
sound imparts to our body ?

Thus, when we speak of the intensity of a
sound of medium force as a magnitude, we allude
principally to the greater or less effort
Intensity and
pitch. The   which we should have ourselves to
part played by
muscular ef-   expend in order to summon, by our
fort.   own effort, the same auditory sensation.
Now, besides the intensity, we distinguish another
characteristic property of the sound, its pitch.

[1] *Grundzüge der Physiologischen Psychologie,* 2nd ed.,
(1880), Vol. ii, p. 437.

Are the differences in pitch, such as our ear
perceives, quantitative differences ? I grant that
a sharper sound calls up the picture of a higher
position in space. But does it follow from
this that the notes of the scale, as auditory
sensations, differ otherwise than in quality ?
Forget what you have learnt from physics, examine carefully your idea of a higher or lower note,
and see whether you do not think simply of the
greater or less effort which the tensor muscle
of your vocal chords has to make in order to
produce the note ? As the effort by which your
voice passes from one note to another is discontinuous, you picture to yourself these successive
notes as points in space, to be reached by a series
of sudden jumps, in each of which you cross an
empty separating interval : this is why you
establish intervals between the notes of the scale.
Now, why is the line along which we dispose
them vertical rather than horizontal, and why
do we say that the sound ascends in some cases
and descends in others? It must be remembered
that the high notes seem to us to produce some
sort of resonance in the head and the deep notes
in the thorax : this perception, whether real or
illusory, has undoubtedly had some effect in
making us reckon the intervals vertically. But
we must also notice that the greater the tension
of the vocal chords in the chest voice, the greater
is the surface of the body affected, if the singer
is inexperienced ; this is just the reason why the

effort is felt by him as more intense. And as he breathes out the air upwards, he will attribute the same direction to the sound produced by the current of air ; hence the sympathy of a larger part of the body with the vocal muscles will be represented by a movement upwards. We shall thus say that the note is higher because the body makes an effort as though to reach an object which is more elevated in space. In this way it became customary to assign a certain height to each note of the scale, and as soon as the physicist was able to define it by the number of vibrations in a given time to which it corresponds, we no longer hesitated to declare that our ear perceived differences of quantity directly. But the sound would remain a pure quality if we did not bring in the muscular effort which produces it or the vibrations which explain it.

The experiments of Blix, Goldscheider and Donaldson [1] have shown that the points on the surface of the body which feel cold are not the same as those which feel heat. Physiology is thus disposed to set up a distinction of nature, and not merely of degree, between the sensations of heat and cold. But psychological observation goes further, for close attention can easily discover specific differences between the different sensations of heat, as also between the sensations of

The sensations of heat and cold. These soon become affective and are measured by reactions called forth.

---

[1] " On the Temperature Sense " *Mind*, 1885.

cold.   A more intense heat is really another kind of heat.   We call it more intense because we have experienced this same change a thousand times when we approached nearer and nearer a source of heat, or when a growing surface of our body was affected by it.   Besides, the sensations of heat and cold very quickly become affective and incite us to more or less marked reactions by which we measure their external cause :   hence, we are inclined to set up similar quantitative differences among the sensations which correspond to lower intensities of the cause.   But I shall not insist any further ;   every one must question himself carefully on this point, after making a clean sweep of everything which his past experience has taught him about the cause of his sensations and coming face to face with the sensations themselves.   The result of this examination is likely to be as follows : it will be perceived that the magnitude of a representative sensation depends on the cause having been put into the effect, while the intensity of the affective element depends on the more or less important reactions which prolong the external stimulations and find their way into the sensation itself.

The same thing will be experienced in the case of pressure and even weight.   When you say *The sensations of pressure and weight measured by extent of organism affected.* that a pressure on your hand becomes stronger and stronger, see whether you do not mean that there first was a contact, then a pressure, afterwards a pain, and that this pain itself, after having gone through a series of qualitative changes, has spread further and further over the surrounding region. Look again and see whether you do not bring in the more and more intense, i.e. more and more extended, effort of resistance which you oppose to the external pressure. When the psychophysicist lifts a heavier weight, he experiences, he says, an increase of sensation. Examine whether this increase of sensation ought not rather to be called a sensation of increase. The whole question is centred in this, for in the first case the sensation would be a quantity like its external cause, whilst in the second it would be a quality which had become representative of the magnitude of its cause. The distinction between the heavy and the light may seem to be as old-fashioned and as childish as that between the hot and the cold. But the very childishness of this distinction makes it a psychological reality. And not only do the heavy and the light impress our consciousness as generically different, but the various degrees of lightness and heaviness are so many species of these two genera. It must be added that the difference of quality is here translated spontaneously into a difference of quantity, because of the more or less extended effort which our body makes in order to lift a given weight. Of this you will soon become aware if you are asked to lift a basket which, you are told, is full of scrap-iron, whilst in fact there is nothing in it. You will think you

are losing your balance when you catch hold of
it, as though distant muscles had interested themselves beforehand in the operation and experienced a sudden disappointment. It is chiefly
by the number and nature of these sympathetic
efforts, which take place at different points of the
organism, that you measure the sensation of
weight at a given point ; and this sensation would
be nothing more than a quality if you did not thus
introduce into it the idea of a magnitude. What
strengthens the illusion on this point is that we
have become accustomed to believe in the immediate perception of a homogeneous movement in a
homogeneous space. When I lift a light weight
with my arm, all the rest of my body remaining
motionless, I experience a series of muscular sensations each of which has its " local sign," its peculiar shade : it is this series which my consciousness interprets as a continuous movement in space.
If I afterwards lift a heavier weight to the same
height with the same speed, I pass through a new
series of muscular sensations, each of which differs
from the corresponding term of the preceding
series. Of this I could easily convince myself
by examining them closely. But as I interpret
this new series also as a continuous movement,
and as this movement has the same direction, the
same duration and the same velocity as the preceding, my consciousness feels itself bound to
localize the difference between the second series
of sensations and the first elsewhere than in the

E

movement itself. It thus materializes this difference at the extremity of the arm which moves ;
it persuades itself that the sensation of movement
has been identical in both cases, while the sensation of weight differed in magnitude. But movement and weight are but distinctions of the reflective consciousness : what is present to consciousness immediately is the sensation of, so to speak,
a heavy movement, and this sensation itself can
be resolved by analysis into a series of muscular
sensations, each of which represents by its shade
its place of origin and by its colour the magnitude
of the weight lifted.

Shall we call the intensity of light a quantity, or
shall we treat it as a quality ? It has not perhaps
been sufficiently noticed what a large
number of different factors co-operate in
daily life in giving us information about
the nature of the luminous source. We
know from long experience that, when we
have a difficulty in distinguishing the
outlines and details of objects, the light
is at a distance or on the point of going out.
Experience has taught us that the affective sensation or nascent dazzling that we experience in certain cases must be attributed to a higher intensity
of the cause. Any increase or diminution in the
number of luminous sources alters the way in
which the sharp lines of bodies stand out and also
the shadows which they project. Still more
important are the changes of hue which coloured

The sensation of light. Qualitative changes of colour interpreted as quantitative changes in intensity of luminous source.

surfaces, and even the pure colours of the spectrum, undergo under the influence of a brighter
or dimmer light. As the luminous source is
brought nearer, violet takes a bluish tinge, green
tends to become a whitish yellow, and red a bril-
liant yellow. Inversely, when the light is moved
away, ultramarine passes into violet and yellow
into green; finally, red, green and violet tend to become a whitish yellow. Physicists have remarked
these changes of hue for some time ;[1] but what
is still more remarkable is that the majority of men
do not perceive them, unless they pay attention to
them or are warned of them. Having made up
our mind, once for all, to interpret changes of
quality as changes of quantity, we begin by asserting that every object has its own peculiar colour,
definite and invariable. And when the hue of
objects tends to become yellow or blue, instead of
saying that we see their colour change under the
influence of an increase or diminution of light, we
assert that the colour remains the same but that
our sensation of luminous intensity increases or
diminishes. We thus substitute once more, for
the qualitative impression received by our consciousness, the quantitative interpretation given
by our understanding. Helmholtz has described
a case of interpretation of the same kind, but still
more complicated : " If we form white with two
colours of the spectrum, and if we increase or

[1] Rood, *Modern Chromatics*, (1879), pp. 181–187.

diminish the intensities of the two coloured lights in the same ratio, so that the proportions of the combination remain the same, the resultant colour remains the same although the relative intensity of the sensations undergoes a marked change. . . . This depends on the fact that the light of the sun, which we consider as the normal white light during the day, itself undergoes similar modifications of shade when the luminous intensity varies." [1]

But yet, if we often judge of variations in the luminous source by the relative changes of hue of the objects which surround us, this is no longer the case in simple instances where a single object, e.g. a white surface, passes successively through different degrees of luminosity. We are bound to insist particularly on this last point. For the physicist speaks of degrees of luminous intensity as of real quantities : and, in fact, he measures them by the photometer. The psychophysicist goes still further : he maintains that our eye itself estimates the intensities of light. Experiments have been attempted, at first by Delbœuf,[2] and afterwards by Lehmann and Neiglick,[3] with

Does experiment prove that we can measure directly our sensations of light?

---

[1] *Handbuch der Physiologischen Optik,* 1st ed. (1867), pp. 318-319.

[2] *Éléments de psychophysique.* Paris, 1883.

[3] See the account given of these experiments in the *Revue philosophique,* 1887, Vol. i, p. 71, and Vol. ii, p. 180.

the view of constructing a psychophysical formula from the direct measurement of our luminous sensations. Of these experiments we shall not dispute the result, nor shall we deny the value of photometric processes ; but we must see how we have to interpret them.

Look closely at a sheet of paper lighted e.g. by four candles, and put out in succession one, two, three of them. You say that the surface remains white and that its brightness diminishes. But you are aware that one candle has just been put out ; or, if you do not know it, you have often observed a similar change in the appearance of a white surface when the illumination was diminished. Put aside what you remember of your past experiences and what you are accustomed to say of the present ones ; you will find that what you really perceive is not a diminished illumination of the white surface, it is a *layer of shadow* passing over this surface at the moment the candle is extinguished. This shadow is a reality to your consciousness, like the light itself. If you call the first surface in all its brilliancy white, you will have to give another name to what you now see, for it is a different thing : it is, if we may say so, a new shade of white. We have grown accustomed, through the combined influence of our past experience and of physical theories, to regard black as the absence, or at least as the minimum, of luminous sensation, and the succes-

Photometric experiments. We perceive different shades and afterwards interpret them as decreasing intensities of white light.

sive shades of grey as decreasing intensities of white light. But, in point of fact, black has just as much reality for our consciousness as white, and the decreasing intensities of white light illuminating a given surface would appear to an unprejudiced consciousness as so many different shades, not unlike the various colours of the spectrum. This is the reason why the change in the sensation is not continuous, as it is in the external cause, and why the light can increase or decrease for a certain period without producing any apparent change in the illumination of our white surface : the illumination will not appear to change until the increase or decrease of the external light is sufficient to produce a new quality. The variations in brightness of a given colour—the affective sensations of which we have spoken above being left aside—would thus be nothing but qualitative changes, were it not our custom to transfer the cause to the effect and to replace our immediate impressions by what we learn from experience and science. The same thing might be said of degrees of saturation. Indeed, if the different intensities of a colour correspond to so many different shades existing between this colour and black, the degrees of saturation are like shades intermediate between this same colour and pure white. Every colour, we might say, can be regarded under two aspects, from the point of view of black and from the point of view of white. And black is then to intensity what white is to saturation.

The meaning of the photometric experiments will now be understood. A candle placed at a certain distance from a sheet of paper illuminates it in a certain way : you double the distance and find that four candles are required to produce the same sensation. From this you conclude that if you had doubled the distance without increasing the intensity of the luminous source, the resultant illumination would have been only one-fourth as bright. But it is quite obvious that you are here dealing with the physical and not the psychological effect. For it cannot be said that you have compared two sensations with one another : you have made use of a single sensation in order to compare two different luminous sources with each other, the second four times as strong as the first but twice as far off. In a word, the physicist never brings in sensations which are twice or three times as great as others, but only identical sensations, destined to serve as intermediaries between two physical quantities which can then be equated with one another. The sensation of light here plays the part of the auxiliary unknown quantity which the mathematician introduces into his calculations, and which is not intended to appear in the final result.

In photometric experiments the physicist compares, not sensations, but physical effects.

But the object of the psychophysicist is entirely different : it is the sensation of light itself which he studies, and claims to measure. Sometimes he will proceed to integrate infinitely small

differences, after the method of Fechner ; sometimes he will compare one sensation
directly with another. The latter
method, due to Plateau and Delbœuf,
differs far less than has hitherto been
believed from Fechner's : but, as it bears
more especially on the luminous sensations, we shall
deal with it first. Delbœuf places an observer
in front of three concentric rings which vary in
brightness. By an ingenious arrangement he can
cause each of these rings to pass through all the
shades intermediate between white and black.
Let us suppose that two hues of grey are simultaneously produced on two of the rings and kept
unchanged ; let us call them A and B. Delbœuf
alters the brightness, C, of the third ring, and asks
the observer to tell him whether, at a certain
moment, the grey, B, appears to him equally distant from the other two. A moment comes, in
fact, when the observer states that the contrast
A B is equal to the contrast B C, so that, according
to Delbœuf, a scale of luminous intensities could
be constructed on which we might pass from each
sensation to the following one by equal sensible
contrasts : our sensations would thus be measured
by one another. I shall not follow Delbœuf
into the conclusions which he has drawn from
these remarkable experiments : the essential question, the only question, as it seems to me, is whether
a contrast A B, formed of the elements A and B, is
really equal to a contrast B C, which is differently

composed.   As soon as it is proved that two sensations can be equal without being identical, psychophysics will be established.   But it is this
equality which seems to me open to question : it
is easy to explain, in fact, how a sensation of
luminous intensity can be said to be at an equal
distance from two others.

Let us assume for a moment that from our birth
onwards the growing intensity of a luminous source
In what case had always called up in our conscious-
differences of
colour might ness, one after the other, the different
be interpreted
as differences colours of the spectrum.   There is no
of magnitude. doubt that these colours would then
appear to us as so many notes of a gamut, as
higher or lower degrees in a scale, in a word, as
magnitudes.   Moreover it would be easy for us to
assign each of them its place in the series.   For
although the extensive cause varies continuously,
the changes in the sensation of colour are discontinuous, passing from one shade to another shade.
However numerous, then, may be the shades intermediate between the two colours, A and B, it
will always be possible to count them in thought,
at least roughly, and ascertain whether this number is almost equal to that of the shades which
separate B from another colour C.   In the latter
case it will be said that B is equally distant from
A and C, that the contrast is the same on one
side as on the other.   But this will always be
merely a convenient interpretation : for although
the number of intermediate shades may be equal

on both sides, although we may pass from one to the other by sudden leaps, we do not know whether these leaps are magnitudes, still less whether they are *equal* magnitudes : above all it would be necessary to show that the intermediaries which have helped us throughout our measurement could be found again inside the object which we have measured. If not, it is only by a metaphor that a sensation can be said to be an equal distance from two others.

Now, if the views which we have before enumerated with regard to luminous intensities are This is just the accepted, it will be recognized that the case with dif- different hues of grey which Delbœuf ferenoes of in- tensity in sen- displays to us are strictly analogous, sations of light. for our consciousness, to colours, and Delbœuf's underlying that if we declare that a grey tint is postulate. equi-distant from two other grey tints, it is in the same sense in which it might be said that orange, for example, is at an equal distance from green and red. But there is this difference, that in all our past experience the succession of grey tints has been produced in connexion with a progressive increase or decrease in illumination. Hence we do for the differences of brightness what we do not think of doing for the differences of colour : we promote the changes of quality into variations of magnitude. Indeed, there is no difficulty here about the measuring, because the successive shades of grey produced by a continuous decrease of illumination are discontinuous, as being

qualities, and because we can count approximately
the principal intermediate shades which separate
any two kinds of grey. The contrast A B will
thus be declared equal to the contrast B C when
our imagination, aided by our memory, inserts
between A and B the same number of intermediate
shades as between B and C. It is needless to say
that this will necessarily be a very rough estimate.
We may anticipate that it will vary considerably
with different persons. Above all it is to be ex-
pected that the person will show more hesitation
and that the estimates of different persons will
differ more widely in proportion as the difference
in brightness between the rings A and B is increased,
for a more and more laborious effort will be required
to estimate the number of intermediate hues.
This is exactly what happens, as we shall easily
perceive by glancing at the two tables drawn up
by Delbœuf.[1] In proportion as he increases the
difference in brightness between the exterior
ring and the middle ring, the difference between
the numbers on which one and the same observer
or different observers successively fix increases
almost continuously from 3 degrees to 94, from
5 to 73, from 10 to 25, from 7 to 40. But let
us leave these divergences on one side : let
us assume that the observers are always consistent and always agree with one another ; will it
then be established that the contrasts A B and
B C are equal ? It would first be necessary to

---

[1] *Eléments de psychophysique*, pp. 61, 69.

prove that two successive elementary contrasts
are equal quantities, whilst, in fact, we only know
that they are successive. It would then be necessary to prove that inside a given tint of grey we
perceive the less intense shades which our imagination has run through in order to estimate the
objective intensity of the source of light. In a
word, Delbœuf's psychophysics assumes a theoretical postulate of the greatest importance,
which is disguised under the cloak of an experimental result, and which we should formulate as
follows : " When the objective quantity of light
is continuously increased, the differences between
the hues of grey successively obtained, each of
which represents the smallest perceptible increase
of physical stimulation, are quantities equal to one
another. And besides, any one of the sensations
obtained can be equated with the sum of the
differences which separate from one another all
previous sensations, going from zero upwards."
Now, this is just the postulate of Fechner's psychophysics, which we are going to examine.

Fechner took as his starting-point a law
discovered by Weber, according to which, given
a certain stimulus which calls forth
a certain sensation, the amount by
which the stimulus must be increased
for consciousness to become aware of any change
bears a fixed relation to the original stimulus.
Thus, if we denote by E the stimulus which
corresponds to the sensation S, and by ΔE

*Fechner's psy-
chophysics.
Weber's Law.*

the amount by which the original stimulus must be increased in order that a sensation of difference may be produced, we shall have $\frac{\Delta E}{E} = const.$

This formula has been much modified by the disciples of Fechner, and we prefer to take no part in the discussion ; it is for experiment to decide between the relation established by Weber and its substitutes. Nor shall we raise any difficulty about granting the probable existence of a law of this nature. It is here really a question not of measuring a sensation but only of determining the exact moment at which an increase of stimulus produces a change in it. Now, if a definite amount of stimulus produces a definite shade of sensation, it is obvious that the minimum amount of stimulus required to produce a change in this shade is also definite ; and since it is not constant, it must be a function of the original stimulus. But how are we to pass from a relation between the stimulus and its minimum increase to an equation which connects the " amount of sensation " with the corresponding stimulus ? The whole of psychophysics is involved in this transition, which is therefore worthy of our closest consideration.

We shall distinguish several different artifices The underlying assumptions and the process by which Fechner's Law is reached. in the process of transition from Weber's experiments, or from any other series of similar observations, to a psychophysical law like Fechner's. It is first of all agreed to consider our consciousness of an increase of stimulus as an increase of the sensation S : this is therefore called S. It is the n asserted that all the sensations ΔS, which correspond to the smallest perceptible increase of stimulus, are equal to one another. They are therefore treated as quantities, and while, on the one hand, these quantities are supposed to be always equal, and, on the other, experiment has given a certain relation ΔE $= f$ (E) between the stimulus E and its minimum increase, the constancy of ΔS is expressed by writing $\Delta S = C \dfrac{\Delta E}{f(E)}$, C being a constant quantity. Finally it is agreed to replace the very small differences ΔS and ΔE by the infinitely small differences dS and dE, whence an equation which is, this time, a differential one : $d S = C \dfrac{d E}{f(E)}$. We shall now simply have to integrate on both sides to obtain the desired relation[1]: $S = C \int_{0}^{E} \dfrac{d E}{f(E)}$. And the transition will thus be made from a proved law, which only concerned the *occurrence* of a sensation, to an unprovable law which gives its *measure*.

Without entering upon any thorough discussion

---

[1] In the particular case where we admit without restriction Weber's Law $\dfrac{\Delta E}{E} = const.$, integration gives $S = C \log. \dfrac{E}{Q}$, Q being a constant. This is Fechner's " logarithmic law."

of this ingenious operation, let us show in a few words how Fechner has grasped the real difficulty of the problem, how he has tried to overcome it, and where, as it seems to us, the flaw in his reasoning lies.

Fechner realized that measurement could not be introduced into psychology without first defining what is meant by the equality and addition of two simple states, e.g. two sensations. But, unless they are identical, we do not at first see how two sensations can be equal. Undoubtedly in the physical world equality is not synonymous with identity. But the reason is that every phenomenon, every object, is there presented under two aspects, the one qualitative and the other extensive : nothing prevents us from putting the first one aside, and then there remains nothing but terms which can be directly or indirectly superposed on one another and consequently seen to be identical. Now, this qualitative element, which we begin by eliminating from external objects in order to measure them, is the very thing which psychophysics retains and claims to measure. And it is no use trying to measure this quality Q by some physical quantity Q' which lies beneath it : for it would be necessary to have previously shown that Q is a function of Q', and this would not be possible unless the quality Q had first been measured with some fraction of itself. Thus nothing prevents us from measuring the sensation of heat by

Can two sensations be equal without being identical ?

the degree of temperature ; but this is only a convention, and the whole point of psychophysics lies in rejecting this convention and seeking how the sensation of heat varies when you change the temperature. In a word, it seems, on the one hand, that two different sensations cannot be said to be equal unless some identical residuum remains after the elimination of their qualitative difference ; but, on the other hand, this qualitative difference being all that we perceive, it does not appear what could remain once it was eliminated.

The novel feature in Fechner's treatment is that he did not consider this difficulty insurmountable. Taking advantage of the fact that sensation varies by sudden jumps while the stimulus increases continuously, he did not hesitate to call these differences of sensation by the same name : they are all, he says, *minimum* differences, since each corresponds to the smallest perceptible increase in the external stimulus. Therefore you can set aside the specific shade or quality of these successive differences ; a common residuum will remain in virtue of which they will be seen to be in a manner identical : they all have the common character of being *minima*. Such will be the definition of equality which we were seeking. Now, the definition of addition will follow naturally. For if we treat as a quantity the difference perceived by consciousness between two sensations which succeed one another in the course of a continuous increase

Fechner's method of *minimum* differences.

of stimulus, if we call the first sensation S, and the second S+ΔS, we shall have to consider every sensation S as a sum, obtained by the addition of the minimum differences through which we pass before reaching it. The only remaining step will then be to utilize this twofold definition in order to establish, first of all, a relation between the differences ΔS and ΔE, and then, through the substitution of the differentials, between the two variables. True, the mathematicians may here lodge a protest against the substitution of differential for difference ; the psychologists may ask, too, whether the quantity ΔS, instead of being constant, does not vary as the sensation S itself ;[1] finally, taking the psychophysical law for granted, we may all debate about its real meaning. But, by the mere fact that ΔS is regarded as a quantity and S as a sum, the fundamental postulate of the whole process is accepted.

Now it is just this postulate which seems to us open to question, even if it can be understood. Assume that I experience a sensation S, and that, increasing the stimulus continuously, I perceive this increase after a certain time. I am now notified of the increase of the cause : but why should I call this notification an arithmetical difference ? No doubt the notification consists in the fact that the original state S has changed :

Break-down of the assumption that the sensation is a sum, and the minimum differences quantities.

---

[1] Latterly it has been assumed that ΔS is proportional to S.

it has become S'; but the transition from S to S'
could only be called an arithmetical difference
if I were conscious, so to speak, of an interval
between S and S', and if my sensation were felt
to rise from S to S' by the addition of something.
By giving this transition a name, by calling it ΔS,
you make it first a reality and then a quantity.
Now, not only are you unable to explain in what
sense this transition is a quantity, but reflection
will show you that it is not even a reality; the
only realities are the states S and S' through which
I pass. No doubt, if S and S' were numbers,
I could assert the reality of the difference S'—S
even though S and S' alone were given; the
reason is that the number S'—S, which is a certain
sum of units, will then represent just the successive
moments of the addition by which we pass from
S to S'. But if S and S' are simple states, in
what will the *interval* which separates them consist? And what, then, can the transition from
the first state to the second be, if not a mere act
of your thought, which, arbitrarily and for the
sake of the argument, assimilates a succession of
two states to a differentiation of two magnitudes?

Either you keep to what consciousness presents
to you or you have recourse to a conventional
We can speak mode of representation. In the first
of "arithme-
tical differ- case you will find a difference between
ence" only in S and S' like that between the shades
a conventional
sense. of the rainbow, and not at all an interval
of magnitude. In the second case you may intro-

duce the symbol ΔS if you like, but it is only in a conventional sense that you will speak here of an arithmetical difference, and in a conventional sense, also, that you will assimilate a sensation to a sum. The most acute of Fechner's critics, Jules Tannery, has made the latter point perfectly clear. "It will be said, for example, that a sensation of 50 degrees is expressed by the number of differential sensations which would succeed one another from the point where sensation is absent up to the sensation of 50 degrees. . . . I do not see that this is anything but a definition, which is as legitimate as it is arbitrary." [1]

We do not believe, in spite of all that has been said, that the method of mean gradations has set psychophysics on a new path. The novel feature in Delbœuf's investigation was that he chose a particular case, in which consciousness seemed to decide in Fechner's favour, and in which common sense itself played the part of the psychophysicist. He inquired whether certain sensations did not appear to us immediately as equal although different, and whether it would not be possible to draw up, by their help, a table of sensations which were double, triple or quadruple those which preceded them. The mistake which Fechner made, as we have just seen, was that he believed in an interval between two successive

Delbœuf's results seem more plausible, but, in the end, all psychophysics revolves in a vicious circle.

---

[1] *Revue scientifique*, March 13 and April 24, 1875.

sensations S and S', when there is simply a *passing* from one to the other and not a *difference* in the arithmetical sense of the word. But if the two terms between which the passing takes place could be given simultaneously, there would then be a contrast besides the transition ; and although the contrast is not yet an arithmetical difference, it resembles it in a certain respect ; for the two terms which are compared stand here side by side as in a case of subtraction of two numbers. Suppose now that these sensations belong to the same *genus* and that in our past experience we have constantly been present at their march past, so to speak, while the physical stimulus increased continuously : it is extremely probable that we shall thrust the cause into the effect, and that the idea of contrast will thus melt into that of arithmetical difference. As we shall have noticed, moreover, that the sensation changed abruptly while the stimulus rose continuously, we shall no doubt estimate the distance between two given sensations by a rough guess at the number of these sudden jumps, or at least of the intermediate sensations which usually serve us as landmarks. To sum up, the contrast will appear to us as a difference, the stimulus as a quantity, the sudden jump as an element of equality : combining these three factors, we shall reach the idea of equal quantitative differences. Now, these conditions are nowhere so well realized as when surfaces of the same colour, more or less illuminated, are simultaneously presented to us. Not only is there here a contrast between similar sensations, but these sensations correspond to a cause whose influence has always been felt by us to be closely connected with its distance ; and, as this distance can vary continuously, we cannot have escaped noticing in our past experience a vast number of shades of sensation which succeeded one another along with the continuous increase in the cause. We are therefore able to say that the contrast between one shade of grey and another, for example, seems to us almost equal to the contrast between the latter and a third one ; and if we define two equal sensations by saying that they are sensations which a more or less confused process of reasoning interprets as such, we shall in fact reach a law like that proposed by Delbœuf. But it must not be forgotten that consciousness has here passed through the same intermediate steps as the psychophysicist, and that its judgment is worth here just what psychophysics is worth ; it is a symbolical interpretation of quality as quantity, a more or less rough estimate of the number of sensations which can come in between two given sensations. The difference is thus not as great as is believed between the method of least noticeable differences and that of mean gradations, between the psychophysics of Fechner and that of Delbœuf. The first led to a conventional measurement of sensation ; the second appeals to common sense in the particular cases where common sense adopts a similar convention. In a word, all psychophysics is condemned by its origin to revolve in a vicious circle, for the theoretical postulate on which it rests condemns it to experimental verification, and it cannot be experimentally verified unless its postulate is first granted. The fact is that there is no point of contact between the unextended and the extended, between quality and quantity. We can interpret the one by the other, set up the one as the equivalent of the other ; but sooner or later, at the beginning or at the end, we shall have to recognize the conventional character of this assimilation.

In truth, psychophysics merely formulates with precision and pushes to its extreme consequences a conception familiar to common sense. As speech dominates over thought, as external objects, which are common to us all, are more important to us than the subjective states through which each of us passes, we have everything to gain by objectifying these states, by introducing into them, to the largest possible extent, the representation of their external cause. And the more our knowledge increases, the more we perceive the extensive behind the intensive, quantity behind quality, the more also we tend to thrust the former into the latter, and to treat our sensations as magnitudes. Physics, whose particular function it is to calculate the external cause of our internal states, takes the least possible interest in these states themselves : constantly and deliberately it confuses them with their cause. It thus encourages and even exaggerates the mistake which common sense makes on the point. The moment was inevitably bound to come at which science, familiarized with this confusion between quality and quantity, between sensation and stimulus, should seek to measure the one as it measures the other : such was the object of psychophysics. In this bold attempt Fechner was encouraged by his adversaries themselves, by the philosophers who speak of intensive magnitudes while declaring that psychic states cannot be submitted to measurement. For if we grant that one sensation can be stronger than another, and that this inequality is inherent in the sensations themselves, independently of all association of ideas, of all more or less conscious consideration of number and space, it is natural to ask by how much the first sensation exceeds the second, and to set up a quantitative relation between their intensities. Nor is it any use to reply, as the opponents of psychophysics sometimes do, that all measurement implies superposition, and that there is no occasion to seek for a numerical relation between intensities, which are not superposable objects. For it will then be necessary to explain why one sensation is said to be more intense than another, and how the conceptions of greater and smaller can be applied to things which, it has just been acknowledged, do not admit among themselves of the relations of container to contained. If, in order to cut short any question of this kind, we distinguish two kinds of quantity, the one intensive, which admits only of a " more or less," the other extensive, which lends itself to measurement, we are not far from siding with Fechner and the psychophysicists. For, as soon as a thing is acknowledged to be capable of increase and decrease, it seems natural to ask by how much it decreases or by how much it increases. And, because a measurement of this kind does not appear to be possible directly, it does not follow that science cannot successfully accomplish it by some indirect process, either by an integration of infinitely small elements, as Fechner proposes, or by any other roundabout way. Either, then, sensation is pure quality, or, if it is a magnitude, we ought to try to measure it.

To sum up what precedes, we have found the notion of intensity to present itself under a double

Thus intensity judged (1) in representative states by an estimate of the magnitude of the cause (2) in affective states by multiplicity of psychic phenomena involved.

aspect, according as we study the states of consciousness which represent an external cause, or those which are self-sufficient. In the former case the perception of intensity consists in a certain estimate of the magnitude of the cause by means of a certain quality in the effect : it is, as the Scottish philosophers would have said, an acquired perception. In the second case, we give the name of intensity to the larger or smaller number of simple psychic phenomena which we conjecture to be involved in the fundamental state : it is no longer an *acquired* perception, but a *confused* perception. In fact, these two meanings of the word usually intermingle, because the simpler phenomena involved in an emotion or an effort are generally representative, and because the majority of representative states, being at the same time affective, themselves include a multiplicity of elementary psychic phenomena. The idea of intensity is thus situated at the junction of two streams, one of which brings us the idea of extensive magnitude from without, while the other brings us from within, in fact from the very depths of consciousness, the image of an inner multiplicity. Now, the point is to determine in what the latter image consists, whether it is the same as that of number, or whether it is quite different from it. In the following chapter we shall no longer consider states of consciousness in isolation from one another, but in their concrete multiplicity, in so far as they unfold themselves in pure duration. And, in the same way as we have asked what would be the intensity of a representative sensation if we did not introduce into it the idea of its cause, we shall now have to inquire what the multiplicity of our inner states becomes, what form duration assumes, when the space in which it unfolds is eliminated. This second question is even more important than the first. For, if the confusion of quality with quantity were confined to each of the phenomena of consciousness taken separately, it would give rise to obscurities, as we have just seen, rather than to problems. But by invading the series of our psychic states, by introducing space into our perception of duration, it corrupts at its very source our feeling of outer and inner change, of movement, and of freedom. Hence the paradoxes of the Eleatics, hence the problem of free will. We shall insist rather on the second point ; but instead of seeking to solve the question, we shall show the mistake of those who ask it.

CHAPTER II

THE MULTIPLICITY OF CONSCIOUS STATES [1]
THE IDEA OF DURATION

NUMBER may be defined in general as a collection of units, or, speaking more exactly, as the synthesis
What is number? of the one and the many. Every number is one, since it is brought before the

---

[1] I had already completed the present work when I read in the *Critique philosophique* (for 1883 and 1884) F. Pillon's very remarkable refutation of an interesting article by G. Noël on the interconnexion of the notions of number and space. But I have not found it necessary to make any alterations in the following pages, seeing that Pillon does not distinguish between time as quality and time as quantity, between the multiplicity of juxtaposition and that of interpenetration. Without this vital distinction, which it is the chief aim of the present chapter to establish, it would be possible to maintain, with Pillon, that number may be built up from the relation of co-existence. But what is here meant by co-existence? If the co-existing terms form an organic whole, they will never lead us to the notion of number; if they remain distinct, they are in juxtaposition and we are dealing with space. It is no use to quote the example of simultaneous impressions received by several senses. We either leave these sensations their specific differences, which amounts to saying that we do not count them; or else we eliminate their differences, and then how are we to distinguish them if not by their position or that of their symbols? We shall see that the verb " to distinguish " has two meanings, the one qualitative, the other

mind by a simple intuition and is given a name ; but the unity which attaches to it is that of a sum, it covers a multiplicity of parts which can be considered separately. Without attempting for the present any thorough examination of these conceptions of unity and multiplicity, let us inquire whether the idea of number does not imply the representation of something else as well.

It is not enough to say that number is a collection of units ; we must add that these units are identical with one another, or at least that they are assumed to be identical when they are counted. No doubt we can count the sheep in a flock and say that there are fifty, although they are all different from one another and are easily recognized by the shepherd : but the reason is that we agree in that case to neglect their individual differences and to take into account only what they have in common. On the other hand, as soon as we fix our attention on the particular features of objects or individuals, we can of course make an enumeration of them, but not a total. We place ourselves at these two very different points of view when we count the soldiers in a battalion and when we call the roll. Hence we may conclude that the idea of number implies the simple intuition of a multiplicity of parts or units, which are absolutely alike.

The units which make up a number must be identical.

quantitative : these two meanings have been confused, in my opinion, by the philosophers who have dealt with the relations between number and space.

And yet they must be somehow distinct from
one another, since otherwise they would merge
into a single unit.   Let us assume that
But they must also be distinct. all the sheep in the flock are identical ;
they differ at least by the position which
they occupy in space, otherwise they would not
form a flock.   But now let us even set aside the
fifty sheep themselves and retain only the idea
of them.   Either we include them all in the same
image, and it follows as a necessary consequence
that we place them side by side in an ideal space,
or else we repeat fifty times in succession the
image of a single one, and in that case it does
seem, indeed, that the series lies in duration
rather than in space.   But we shall soon find out
that it cannot be so.   For if we picture to ourselves
each of the sheep in the flock in succession and
separately, we shall never have to do with more
than a single sheep.   In order that the number
should go on increasing in proportion as we
advance, we must retain the successive images
and set them alongside each of the new units
which we picture to ourselves : now, it is in space
that such a juxtaposition takes place and not in
pure duration.   In fact, it will be easily granted
that counting material objects means thinking all
these objects together, thereby leaving them in
space.   But does this intuition of space accompany every idea of number, even of an abstract
number ?

Any one can answer this question by reviewing

the various forms which the idea of number has

assumed for him since his childhood. It will be seen that we began by imagining e.g. a row of balls, that these balls afterwards became points, and, finally, this image itself disappeared, leaving behind it, as we say, nothing but *abstract* number. But at this very moment we ceased to have an image or even an idea of it ; we kept only the symbol which is necessary for reckoning and which is the conventional way of *expressing* number. For we can confidently assert that 12 is half of 24 without thinking either the number 12 or the number 24 : indeed, as far as quick calculation is concerned, we have everything to gain by not doing so. But as soon as we wish to picture *number* to ourselves, and not merely figures or words, we are compelled to have recourse to an extended image. What leads to misunderstanding on this point seems to be the habit we have fallen into of counting in time rather than in space. In order to imagine the number 50, for example, we repeat all the numbers starting from unity, and when we have arrived at the fiftieth, we believe we have built up the number in duration and in duration only. And there is no doubt that in this way we have counted moments of duration rather than points in space ; but the question is whether we have not counted the moments of duration by means of points in space. It is certainly possible to perceive in time, and in time only, a succession which is nothing but a succession, but not an addition, i.e. a succession which culminates in a sum. For though we reach a sum by taking into account a succession of different terms, yet it is necessary that each of these terms should remain when we pass to the following, and should wait, so to speak, to be added to the others : how could it wait, if it were nothing but an instant of duration ? And where could it wait if we did not localize it in space ? We involuntarily fix at a point in space each of the moments which we count, and it is only on this condition that the abstract units come to form a sum. No doubt it is possible, as we shall show later, to conceive the successive moments of time independently of space ; but when we add to the present moment those which have preceded it, as is the case when we are adding up units, we are not dealing with these moments themselves, since they have vanished for ever, but with the lasting traces which they seem to have left in space on their passage through it. It is true that we generally dispense with this mental image, and that, after having used it for the first two or three numbers, it is enough to know that it would serve just as well for the mental picturing of the others, if we needed it. But every clear idea of number implies a visual image in space ; and the direct study of the units which go to form a discrete multiplicity will lead us to the same conclusion on this point as the examination of number itself.

Every number is a collection of units, as we have said, and on the other hand every number is itself a unit, in so far as it is a synthesis of the units which compose it. But is the word *unit* taken in the same sense in both cases ? When we assert that number is a unit, we understand by this that we master the whole of it by a simple and indivisible intuition of the mind ; this unity thus includes a multiplicity, since it is the unity of a whole. But when we speak of the units which go to form number, we no longer think of these units as sums, but as pure, simple, irreducible units, intended to yield the natural series of numbers by an indefinitely continued process of accumulation. It seems, then, that there are two kinds of units, the one ultimate, out of which a number is formed by a process of addition, and the other provisional, the number so formed, which is multiple in itself, and owes its unity to the simplicity of the act by which the mind perceives it. And there is no doubt that, when we picture the units which make up number, we believe that we are thinking of indivisible components : this belief has a great deal to do with the idea that it is possible to conceive number independently of space. Nevertheless, by looking more closely into the matter, we shall see that all unity is the unity of a simple act of the mind, and that, as this is an act of unification, there must be some multiplicity for it to unify. No doubt, at

All unity is the unity of a simple act of the mind. Units divisible only because regarded as extended in space.

the moment at which I think each of these units
separately, I look upon it as <u>indivisible</u>, since I
am determined to think of its unity alone. But
as soon as I put it aside in order to pass to the
next, I objectify it, and by that very deed I make
it a thing, that is to say, a multiplicity. To convince oneself of this, it is enough to notice that
the units by means of which arithmetic forms
numbers are *provisional* units, which can be sub-
divided without limit, and that each of them is
the sum of fractional quantities as small and as
numerous as we like to imagine. How could we
divide the unit, if it were here that ultimate unity
which characterizes a simple act of the mind ?
How could we split it up into fractions whilst
affirming its unity, if we did not regard it implicitly
as an extended object, one in intuition but multiple
in space ? You will never get out of an idea
which you have formed anything which you
have not put into it ; and if the unity by means of
which you make up your number is the unity of
an act and not of an object, no effort of analysis
will bring out of it anything but unity pure and
simple. No doubt, when you equate the number
3 to the sum of $1 + 1 + 1$, nothing prevents you
from regarding the units which compose it as
indivisible : but the reason is that you do not
choose to make use of the multiplicity which is
enclosed within each of these units. Indeed, it
is probable that the number 3 first assumes to
our mind this simpler shape, because we think

rather of the way in which we have obtained it than of the use which we might make of it. But we soon perceive that, while all multiplication implies the possibility of treating any number whatever as a provisional unit which can be added to itself, inversely the units in their turn are true numbers which are as big as we like, but are regarded as provisionally indivisible for the purpose of compounding them with one another. Now, the very admission that it is possible to divide the unit into as many parts as we like, shows that we regard it as extended.

For we must understand what is meant by the *discontinuity* of number. It cannot be denied that the formation or construction of a number implies discontinuity. In other words, as we remarked above, each of the units with which we form the number 3 seems to be indivisible while we are dealing with it, and we pass abruptly from one to the other. Again, if we form the same number with halves, with quarters, with any units whatever, these units, in so far as they serve to form the said number, will still constitute elements which are provisionally indivisible, and it is always by jerks, by sudden jumps, so to speak, that we advance from one to the other. And the reason is that, in order to get a number, we are compelled to fix our attention successively on each of the units of which it is compounded. The indivisibility of the act by which

Number in process of formation is discontinuous, but, when formed, is invested with the continuity of space.

we conceive any one of them is then represented
under the form of a mathematical point which is
separated from the following point by an interval of
space. But, while a series of mathematical points
arranged in empty space expresses fairly well the
process by which we form the idea of number,
these mathematical points have a tendency to
develop into lines in proportion as our attention
is diverted from them, as if they were trying to
reunite with one another. And when we look at
number in its finished state, this union is an accomplished fact : the points have become lines, the
divisions have been blotted out, the whole displays
all the characteristics of continuity. This is why
number, although we have formed it according
to a definite law, can be split up on any system
we please. In a word, we must distinguish between the unity which we think of and the unity
which we set up as an object after having thought
of it, as also between number in process of formation and number once formed. The unit is irreducible while we are thinking it and number is
discontinuous while we are building it up : but,
as soon as we consider number in its finished state,
we objectify it, and it then appears to be divisible
to an unlimited extent. In fact, we apply the
term *subjective* to what seems to be completely
and adequately known, and the term *objective*
to what is known in such a way that a constantly
increasing number of new impressions could be
substituted for the idea which we actually have

of it. Thus, a complex feeling will contain a fairly large number of simple elements ; but, as long as these elements do not stand out with perfect clearness, we cannot say that they were completely realized, and, as soon as consciousness has a distinct perception of them, the psychic state which results from their synthesis will have changed for this very reason. But there is no change in the general appearance of a body, however it is analysed by thought, because these different analyses, and an infinity of others, are already visible in the mental image which we form of the body, though they are not realized : this actual and not merely virtual perception of subdivisions in what is undivided is just what we call objectivity. It then becomes easy to determine the exact part played by the subjective and the objective in the idea of number. What properly belongs to the mind is the indivisible process by which it concentrates attention successively on the different parts of a given space ; but the parts which have thus been isolated remain in order to join with the others, and, once the addition is made, they may be broken up in any way whatever. They are therefore parts of space, and space is, accordingly, the material with which the mind builds up number, the medium in which the mind places it.

Properly speaking, it is arithmetic which teaches us to split up without limit the units of which number consists. Common sense is very much inclined to build up number with indivisibles.

And this is easily understood, since the pro-visional simplicity of the component units is just what they owe to the mind, and the latter pays more attention to its own acts than to the material on which it works. Science confines itself, here, to drawing our attention to this material : if we did not already localize number in space, science would certainly not succeed in making us transfer it thither. From the beginning, therefore, we must have thought of number as of a juxtaposition in space. This is the conclusion which we reached at first, basing ourselves on the fact that all addi-tion implies a multiplicity of parts simultaneously perceived.

It follows that number is actually thought of as a juxtaposition in space.

Now, if this conception of number is granted, it will be seen that everything is not counted in the same way, and that there are two very different kinds of multiplicity. When we speak of material objects, we refer to the possibility of seeing and touching them ; we localize them in space. In that case, no effort of the inventive faculty or of symbolical repre-sentation is necessary in order to count them ; we have only to think them, at first separ-ately, and then simultaneously, within the very medium in which they come under our observation. The case is no longer the same when we consider purely affective psychic states, or even mental

Two kinds of multiplicity : (1) material objects, counted in space ; (2) conscious states, not countable un-less symbolic-ally repre-sented in space.

images other than those built up by means of
sight and touch. Here, the terms being no longer
given in space, it seems, *a priori*, that we can
hardly count them except by some process of
symbolical representation. In fact, we are well
aware of a representation of this kind when
we are dealing with sensations the cause of
which is obviously situated in space. Thus, when
we hear a noise of steps in the street, we have
a confused vision of somebody walking along :
each of the successive sounds is then localized at
a point in space where the passer-by might tread :
we count our sensations in the very space in which
their tangible causes are ranged. Perhaps some
people count the successive strokes of a distant
bell in a similar way, their imagination pictures
the bell coming and going ; this spatial sort of
image is sufficient for the first two units, and the
others follow naturally. But most people's minds
do not proceed in this way. They range the successive sounds in an ideal space and then fancy
that they are counting them in pure duration.
Yet we must be clear on this point. The sounds
of the bell certainly reach me one after the other ;
but one of two alternatives must be true. Either
I retain each of these successive sensations in order
to combine it with the others and form a group
which reminds me of an air or rhythm which I
know : in that case I do not *count* the sounds, I
limit myself to gathering, so to speak, the qualitative impression produced by the whole series. Or

else I intend explicitly to count them, and then I shall have to separate them, and this separation must take place within some homogeneous medium in which the sounds, stripped of their qualities, and in a manner emptied, leave traces of their presence which are absolutely alike. The question now is, whether this medium is time or space. But a moment of time, we repeat, cannot persist in order to be added to others. If the sounds are separated, they must leave empty intervals between them. If we count them, the intervals must remain though the sounds disappear : how could these intervals remain, if they were pure duration and not space ? It is in space, therefore, that the operation takes place. It becomes, indeed, more and more difficult as we penetrate further into the depths of consciousness. Here we find ourselves confronted by a confused multiplicity of sensations and feelings which analysis alone can distinguish. Their number is identical with the number of the moments which we take up when we count them ; but these moments, as they can be added to one another, are again points in space. Our final conclusion, therefore, is that there are two kinds of multiplicity : that of material objects, to which the conception of number is immediately applicable ; and the multiplicity of states of consciousness, which cannot be regarded as numerical without the help of some symbolical representation, in which a necessary element is *space*.

As a matter of fact, each of us makes a distinction between these two kinds of multiplicity **The impenetra-** whenever he speaks of the impenetra-**trability of matter is not a** bility of matter. We sometimes set up **physical but a logical neces-** impenetrability as a fundamental pro-**sity.** perty of bodies, known in the same way and put on the same level as e.g. weight or resistance. But a purely negative property of this kind cannot be revealed by our senses ; indeed, certain experiments in mixing and combining things might lead us to call it in question if our minds were not already made up on the point. Try to picture one body penetrating another : you will at once assume that there are empty spaces in the one which will be occupied by the particles of the other ; these particles in their turn cannot penetrate one another unless one of them divides in order to fill up the interstices of the other ; and our thought will prolong this operation indefinitely in preference to picturing two bodies in the same place. Now, if impenetrability were really a quality of matter which was known by the senses, it is not at all clear why we should experience more difficulty in conceiving two bodies merging into one another than a surface devoid of resistance or a weightless fluid. In reality, it is not a physical but a logical necessity which attaches to the proposition : " Two bodies cannot occupy the same place at the same time." The contrary assertion involves an absurdity which no conceivable experience could succeed in dispelling.

In a word, it implies a contradiction. But does not this amount to recognizing that the very idea of the number 2, or, more generally, of any number whatever, involves the idea of juxtaposition in space ? If impenetrability is generally regarded as a quality of matter, the reason is that the idea of number is thought to be independent of the idea of space. We thus believe that we are adding something to the idea of two or more objects by saying that they cannot occupy the same place : as if the idea of the number 2, even the abstract number, were not already, as we have shown, that of two different positions in space ! Hence to assert the impenetrability of matter is simply to recognize the inter-connexion between the notions of number and space, it is to state a property of number rather than of matter.—Yet, it will be said, do we not count feelings, sensations, ideas, all of which permeate one another, and each of which, for its part, takes up the whole of the soul ?—Yes, undoubtedly ; but, just because they permeate one another, we cannot count them unless we represent them by homogeneous units which occupy separate positions in space and consequently no longer permeate one another. Impenetrability thus makes its appearance at the same time as number ; and when we attribute this quality to matter in order to distinguish it from everything which is not matter, we simply state under another form the distinction established above between extended objects, to which the conception of number is immediately applicable, and states of consciousness, which have first of all to be represented symbolically in space.

It is advisable to dwell on the last point. If, in order to count states of consciousness, we have Homogeneous to represent them symbolically in space, time as the is it not likely that this symbolical repre- which con- sentation will alter the normal con- scious states form discrete ditions of inner perception ? Let us series. This time is no- recall what we said a short time ago thing but space, and about the intensity of certain psychic pure duration is something states. Representative sensation, looked different. at in itself, is pure quality ; but, seen through the medium of extensity, this quality becomes in a certain sense quantity, and is called intensity. In the same way, our projection of our psychic states into space in order to form a discrete multiplicity is likely to influence these states themselves and to give them in reflective consciousness a new form, which immediate perception did not at-tribute to them. Now, let us notice that when we speak of *time*, we generally think of a homo-geneous medium in which our conscious states are ranged alongside one another as in space, so as to form a discrete multiplicity. Would not time, thus understood, be to the multiplicity of our psychic states what intensity is to certain of them, —a sign, a symbol, absolutely distinct from true duration ? Let us ask consciousness to isolate itself from the external world, and, by a vigorous effort of abstraction, to become itself again. We shall then put this question to it : does the multiplicity of our conscious states bear the slightest resemblance to the multiplicity of the units of a number ? Has true duration anything to do with space ? Certainly, our analysis of the idea of number could not but make us doubt this analogy, to say no more. For if time, as the reflective consciousness represents it, is a medium in which our conscious states form a discrete series so as to admit of being counted, and if on the other hand our conception of number ends in spreading out in space everything which can be directly counted, it is to be presumed that time, understood in the sense of a medium in which we make distinctions and count, is nothing but space. That which goes to confirm this opinion is that we are compelled to borrow from space the images by which we describe what the reflective consciousness feels about time and even about succession ; it follows that pure duration must be something different. Such are the questions which we have been led to ask by the very analysis of the notion of discrete multiplicity. But we cannot throw any light upon them except by a direct study of the ideas of space and time in their mutual relations.

We shall not lay too much stress on the question of the absolute reality of space : perhaps we might **Does space exist independently of its contents, as Kant held ?** as well ask whether space is or is not in space. In short, our senses perceive the qualities of bodies and space along

with them : the great difficulty seems to
have been to discover whether extensity is an
aspect of these physical qualities—a quality of
quality—or whether these qualities are essentially
unextended, space coming in as a later addition,
but being self-sufficient and existing without
them. On the first hypothesis, space would be
reduced to an abstraction, or, speaking more
correctly, an extract ; it would express the common element possessed by certain sensations called
representative. In the second case, space would
be a reality as solid as the sensations themselves,
although of a different order. We owe the exact
formulation of this latter conception to Kant :
the theory which he works out in the Transcendental Aesthetic consists in endowing space
with an existence independent of its content, in
laying down as *de jure* separable what each of
us separates *de facto*, and in refusing to regard
extensity as an abstraction like the others. In
this respect the Kantian conception of space differs
less than is usually imagined from the popular belief. Far from shaking our faith in the reality of
space, Kant has shown what it actually means
and has even justified it.

Moreover, the solution given by Kant does not
seem to have been seriously disputed since his
time : indeed, it has forced itself, sometimes
without their knowledge, on the majority of
those who have approached the problem anew,
whether nativists or empiricists. Psychologists

agree in assigning a Kantian origin to the na-
tivistic explanation of Johann Müller ;
but Lotze's hypothesis of local signs,
Bain's theory, and the more comprehensive explanation suggested by Wundt,
may seem at first sight quite independent
of the Transcendental Aesthetic.   The
authors of these theories seem indeed to
have put aside the problem of the nature of space, in
order to investigate simply by what process our
sensations come to be situated in space and to be
set, so to speak, alongside one another : but this
very question shows that they regard sensations
as inextensive and make a radical distinction, just
as Kant did, between the matter of representation
and its form.   The conclusion to be drawn from
the theories of Lotze and Bain, and from Wundt's
attempt to reconcile them, is that the sensations
by means of which we come to form the notion of
space are themselves unextended and simply
qualitative : extensity is supposed to result from
their synthesis, as water from the combination of
two gases.   The empirical or genetic explanations
have thus taken up the problem of space at the
very point where Kant left it : Kant separated
space from its contents : the empiricists ask how
these contents, which are taken out of space by
our thought, manage to get back again.   It is true
that they have apparently disregarded the activity
of the mind, and that they are obviously inclined
to regard the extensive form under which we repre-

The empiri-
cists really
agree with
Kant, for
extensity can-
not result
from synthe-
sis of unex-
tended sensa-
tions without
an act of the
mind.

sent things as produced by a kind of alliance of the sensations with one another: space, without being extracted from the sensations, is supposed to result from their co-existence. But how can we explain such an origination without the active intervention of the mind ? The extensive differs by hypothesis from the inextensive : and even if we assume that extension is nothing but a relation between inextensive terms, this relation must still be established by a mind capable of thus associating several terms. It is no use quoting the example of chemical combinations, in which the whole seems to assume, of its own accord, a form and qualities which did not belong to any of the elementary atoms. This form and these qualities owe their origin just to the fact that we gather up the multiplicity of atoms in a single perception : get rid of the mind which carries out this synthesis and you will at once do away with the qualities, that is to say, the aspect under which the synthesis of elementary parts is presented to our consciousness. Thus inextensive sensations will remain what they are, viz., inextensive sensations, if nothing be added to them. For their co-existence to give rise to space, there must be an act of the mind which takes them in all at the same time and sets them in juxtaposition : this unique act is very like what Kant calls an *a priori* form of sensibility.

If we now seek to characterize this act, we see that it consists essentially in the intuition, or

rather the conception, of an empty homogeneous medium. For it is scarcely
possible to give any other definition of
space : space is what enables us to distinguish a number of identical and
simultaneous sensations from one another; it is thus a principle of differentiation other than that of qualitative differentiation,
and consequently it is a reality with no quality.
Some one may say, with the believers in the theory of
local signs, that simultaneous sensations are never
identical, and that, in consequence of the diversity
of the organic elements which they affect, there
are no two points of a homogeneous surface which
make the same impression on the sight or the
touch. We are quite ready to grant it, for if these
two points affected us in the same way, there would
be no reason for placing one of them on the right
rather than on the left. But, just because we afterwards interpret this difference of quality in the sense
of a difference of situation, it follows that we must
have a clear idea of a homogeneous medium, i.e.
of a simultaneity of terms which, although identical
in quality, are yet distinct from one another. The
more you insist on the difference between the
impressions made on our retina by two points
of a homogeneous surface, the more do you
thereby make room for the activity of the mind,
which perceives under the form of extensive
homogeneity what is given it as qualitative
heterogeneity. No doubt, though the repre-

This act con-
sists in the
intuition of
an empty
homogeneous
medium :
perhaps pecu-
liar to man and
not shared by
animals.

sentation of a homogeneous space grows out of
an effort of the mind, there must be within
the qualities themselves which differentiate two
sensations some reason why they occupy this
or that definite position in space. We must
thus distinguish between the perception of
extensity and the conception of space : they
are no doubt implied in one another, but, the
higher we rise in the scale of intelligent beings,
the more clearly do we meet with the independent
idea of a homogeneous space. It is therefore
doubtful whether animals perceive the external
world quite as we do, and especially whether they
represent externality in the same way as ourselves.
Naturalists have pointed out, as a remarkable
fact, the surprising ease with which many verte-
brates, and even some insects, manage to find their
way through space. Animals have been seen to
return almost in a straight line to their old home,
pursuing a path which was hitherto unknown to
them over a distance which may amount to several
hundreds of miles. Attempts have been made to
explain this feeling of direction by sight or smell,
and, more recently, by the perception of magnetic
currents which would enable the animal to take
its bearings like a living compass. This amounts
to saying that space is not so homogeneous for the
animal as for us, and that determinations of space,
or directions, do not assume for it a purely geometrical form. Each of these directions might appear
to it with its own shade, its peculiar quality. We

shall understand how a perception of this kind is possible if we remember that we ourselves distinguish our right from our left by a natural feeling, and that these two parts of our own extensity do then appear to us as if they bore a different *quality* ; in fact, this is the very reason why we cannot give a proper definition of right and left.   In truth, qualitative differences exist everywhere in nature, and I do not see why two concrete directions should not be as marked in immediate perception as two colours.   But the conception of an empty homogeneous medium is something far more extraordinary, being a kind of reaction against that heterogeneity which is the very ground of our experience. Therefore, instead of saying that animals have a special sense of direction, we may as well say that men have a special faculty of perceiving or conceiving a space without quality.   This faculty is not the faculty of abstraction : indeed, if we notice that abstraction assumes clean-cut distinctions and a kind of externality of the concepts or their symbols with regard to one another, we shall find that the faculty of abstraction already implies the intuition of a homogeneous medium.   What we must say is that we have to do with two different kinds of reality, the one heterogeneous, that of sensible qualities, the other homogeneous, namely space.   This latter, clearly conceived by the human intellect, enables us to use clean-cut distinctions, to count, to abstract, and perhaps also to speak.

H

(?)

Now, if space is to be defined as the homogeneous, it seems that inversely every homogeneous
Time, in so and unbounded medium will be space.
far as it is a For, homogeneity here consisting in the
homogeneous
medium, and absence of every quality, it is hard to
not concrete
duration, is see how two forms of the homogeneous
reducible to
space. could be distinguished from one another.
Nevertheless it is generally agreed to regard time
as an unbounded medium, different from space
but homogeneous like the latter : the homogeneous is thus supposed to take two forms, according
as its contents co-exist or follow one another. It
is true that, when we make time a homogeneous
medium in which conscious states unfold themselves, we take it to be given all at once, which
amounts to saying that we abstract it from duration. This simple consideration ought to warn us
that we are thus unwittingly falling back upon
space, and really giving up time. Moreover, we
can understand that material objects, being exterior to one another and to ourselves, derive both
exteriorities from the homogeneity of a medium
which inserts intervals between them and sets off
their outlines : but states of consciousness, even
when successive, permeate one another, and in the
simplest of them the whole soul can be reflected.
We may therefore surmise that time, conceived
under the form of a homogeneous medium, is
some spurious concept, due to the trespassing of
the idea of space upon the field of pure consciousness. At any rate we cannot finally admit two

forms of the homogeneous, time and space, without first seeking whether one of them cannot be reduced to the other.   Now, externality is the distinguishing mark of things which occupy space, while states of consciousness are not essentially external to one another, and become so only by being spread out in time, regarded as a homogeneous medium.   If, then, one of these two supposed forms of the homogeneous, namely time and space, is derived from the other, we can surmise *a priori* that the idea of space is the fundamental datum. But, misled by the apparent simplicity of the idea of time, the philosophers who have tried to reduce one of these ideas to the other have thought that they could make extensity out of duration.   While showing how they have been misled, we shall see that time, conceived under the form of an unbounded and homogeneous medium, is nothing but the ghost of space haunting the reflective consciousness.

The English school tries, in fact, to reduce relations of extensity to more or less complex relations of succession in time.   When, with our eyes shut, we run our hands along a surface, the rubbing of our fingers against the surface, and especially the varied play of our joints, provide a series of sensations, which differ only by their *qualities* and which exhibit a certain order in time.   Moreover, experience teaches us that this series can be reversed, that we can, by an

Mistake of the attempt to derive relations of extensity from those of succession. The conception of " pure duration."

effort of a different kind (or, as we shall call it
later, *in an opposite direction*), obtain the same
sensations over again in an inverse order : relations
of position in space might then be defined as
reversible relations of succession in time. But
such a definition involves a vicious circle, or at
least a very superficial idea of time.   There are,
indeed, as we shall show a little later, two possible
conceptions of time, the one free from all alloy,
the other surreptitiously bringing in the idea of
space.   Pure duration is the form which the succession of our conscious states assumes when our
ego lets itself *live*, when it refrains from separating its present state from its former states.   For
this purpose it need not be entirely absorbed in the
passing sensation or idea; for then, on the contrary, it would no longer *endure*.   Nor need
it forget its former states : it is enough that,
in recalling these states, it does not set them
alongside its actual state as one point alongside another, but forms both the past and the
present states into an organic whole, as happens
when we recall the notes of a tune, melting,
so to speak, into one another.   Might it not
be said that, even if these notes succeed one
another, yet we perceive them in one another, and
that their totality may be compared to a living
being whose parts, although distinct, permeate
one another just because they are so closely connected ?   The proof is that, if we interrupt the
rhythm by dwelling longer than is right on one

note of the tune, it is not its exaggerated length,
as length, which will warn us of our mistake, but
the qualitative change thereby caused in the
whole of the musical phrase.   We can thus conceive of succession without distinction, and think
of it as a mutual penetration, an interconnexion
and organization of elements, each one of which
represents the whole, and cannot be distinguished
or isolated from it except by abstract thought.
Such is the account of duration which would be
given by a being who was ever the same and ever
changing, and who had no idea of space.   But,
familiar with the latter idea and indeed beset by
it, we introduce it unwittingly into our feeling of
pure succession ; we set our states of consciousness
side by side in such a way as to perceive them
simultaneously, no longer in one another, but
alongside one another ; in a word, we project
time into space, we express duration in terms of
extensity, and succession thus takes the form of a
continuous line or a chain, the parts of which touch
without penetrating one another.   Note that the
mental image thus shaped implies the perception,
no longer successive, but simultaneous, of a *before*
and *after*, and that it would be a contradiction to
suppose a succession which was only a succession,
and which nevertheless was contained in one and
the same instant.   Now, when we speak of an
order of succession in duration, and of the reversi-
bility of this order, is the succession we are dealing
with pure succession, such as we have just defined

it, without any admixture of extensity, or is it succession developing in space, in such a way that we can take in at once a number of elements which are both distinct and set side by side ? There is no doubt about the answer : we could not introduce *order* among terms without first distinguishing them and then comparing the places which they occupy ; hence we must perceive them as multiple, simultaneous and distinct ; in a word, we set them side by side, and if we introduce an order in what is successive, the reason is that succession is converted into simultaneity and is projected into space. In short, when the movement of my finger along a surface or a line provides me with a series of sensations of different qualities, one of two things happens : either I picture these sensations to myself as in duration only, and in that case they succeed one another in such a way that I cannot at a given moment perceive a number of them as simultaneous and yet distinct ; or else I make out an order of succession, but in that case I display the faculty not only of perceiving a succession of elements, but also of setting them out in line after having distinguished them : in a word, I already possess the idea of space. Hence the idea of a reversible series in duration, or even simply of a certain *order* of succession in time, itself implies the representation of space, and cannot be used to define it.

To give this argument a stricter form, let us imagine a straight line of unlimited length, and on this line a material point A, which moves.

Succession cannot be symbolized as a line without introducing the idea of space of three dimensions.
If this point were conscious of itself, it would feel itself change, since it moves : it would perceive a succession; but would this succession assume for it the form of a line ? No doubt it would, if it could rise, so to speak, above the line which it traverses, and perceive simultaneously several points of it in juxtaposition : but by doing so it would form the idea of space, and it is in space and not in pure duration that it would see displayed the changes which it undergoes. We here put our finger on the mistake of those who regard pure duration as something similar to space, but of a simpler nature. They are fond of setting psychic states side by side, of forming a chain or a line of them, and do not imagine that they are introducing into this operation the idea of space properly so called, the idea of space in its totality, because space is a medium of three dimensions. But how can they fail to notice that, in order to perceive a line as a line, it is necessary to take up a position outside it, to take account of the void which surrounds it, and consequently to think a space of three dimensions ? If our conscious point A does not yet possess the idea of space— and this is the hypothesis which we have agreed to adopt—the succession of states through which it passes cannot assume for it the form of a line ; but its sensations will add themselves dynamically to one another and will organize themselves, like

the successive notes of a tune by which we allow ourselves to be lulled and soothed. /In a word, pure duration might well be nothing but a succession of qualitative changes, which melt into and permeate one another, without precise outlines, without any tendency to externalize themselves in relation to one another, without any affiliation with number : it would be pure heterogeneity. But for the present we shall not insist upon this point; it is enough for us to have shown that, from the moment when you attribute the least homogeneity to duration, you surreptitiously introduce space.

It is true that we count successive moments of duration, and that, because of its relations with

Pure duration is wholly qualitative. It cannot be measured unless symbolically represented in space. number, time at first seems to us to be a measurable magnitude, just like space. But there is here an important distinction to be made. I say, e.g., that a minute has just elapsed, and I mean by this that a pendulum, beating the seconds, has completed sixty oscillations. If I picture these sixty oscillations to myself all at once by a single mental perception, I exclude by hypothesis the idea of a succession. I do not think of sixty strokes which succeed one another, but of sixty points on a fixed line, each one of which symbolizes, so to speak, an oscillation of the pendulum. If, on the other hand, I wish to picture these sixty oscillations in succession, but without altering the way they are produced in space, I shall

be compelled to think of each oscillation to the
exclusion of the recollection of the preceding one,
for space has preserved no trace of it ; but by
doing so I shall condemn myself to remain for
ever in the present ; I shall give up the attempt
to think a succession or a duration.   Now if,
finally, I retain the recollection of the preceding
oscillation together with the image of the present
oscillation, one of two things will happen.   Either
I shall set the two images side by side, and we then
fall back on our first hypothesis, or I shall perceive one in the other, each permeating the other and
organizing themselves like the notes of a tune, so
as to form what we shall call a continuous or
qualitative multiplicity with no resemblance to
number.   I shall thus get the image of pure duration ; but I shall have entirely got rid of the idea
of a homogeneous medium or a measurable quantity.   By carefully examining our consciousness
we shall recognize that it proceeds in this way
whenever it refrains from representing duration
symbolically.   When the regular oscillations of the
pendulum make us sleepy, is it the last sound
heard, the last movement perceived, which produces this effect ?   No, undoubtedly not, for why
then should not the first have done the same ?
Is it the recollection of the preceding sounds or
movements, set in juxtaposition to the last one ?
But this same recollection, if it is later on set in
juxtaposition to a single sound or movement, will
remain without effect.   Hence we must admit

that the sounds combined with one another and acted, not by their quantity as quantity, but by the quality which their quantity exhibited, i.e. by the rhythmic organization of the whole. Could the effect of a slight but continuous stimulation be understood in any other way? If the sensation remained always the same, it would continue to be indefinitely slight and indefinitely bearable. But the fact is that each increase of stimulation is taken up into the preceding stimulations, and that the whole produces on us the effect of a musical phrase which is constantly on the point of ending and constantly altered in its totality by the addition of some new note. If we assert that it is always the *same* sensation, the reason is that we are thinking, not of the sensation itself, but of its objective cause situated in space. We then set it out in space in its turn, and in place of an organism which develops, in place of changes which permeate one another, we perceive one and the same sensation stretching itself out lengthwise, so to speak, and setting itself in juxtaposition to itself without limit. Pure duration, that which consciousness perceives, must thus be reckoned among the so-called intensive magnitudes, if intensities can be called magnitudes : strictly speaking, however, it is not a quantity, and as soon as we try to measure it, we unwittingly replace it by space.

But we find it extraordinarily difficult to think of duration in its original purity ; this is due, no doubt, to the fact that we do not *endure*

alone, external objects, it seems, *endure*
as we do, and time, regarded from
this point of view, has every appearance of a homogeneous medium. Not
only do the moments of this duration
seem to be external to one another, like
bodies in space, but the movement perceived by
our senses is the, so to speak, palpable sign of a
homogeneous and measurable duration. Nay
more, time enters into the formulae of mechanics,
into the calculations of the astronomer, and even
of the physicist, under the form of a quantity.
We measure the velocity of a movement, implying
that time itself is a magnitude. Indeed, the
analysis which we have just attempted requires
to be completed, for if duration properly so-called
cannot be measured, what is it that is measured
by the oscillations of the pendulum ? Granted
that inner duration, perceived by consciousness,
is nothing else but the melting of states of
consciousness into one another, and the gradual
growth of the ego, it will be said, notwithstanding,
that the time which the astronomer introduces
into his formulae, the time which our clocks
divide into equal portions, this time, at least, is
something different : it must be a measurable
and therefore homogeneous magnitude.—It is
nothing of the sort, however, and a close examination will dispel this last illusion.

When I follow with my eyes on the dial of a

clock the movement of the hand which corresponds to the oscillations of the pendulum, I do not measure duration, as
seems to be thought ; I merely count
simultaneities, which is very different.
Outside of me, in space, there is never
more than a single position of the hand and
the pendulum, for nothing is left of the
past positions. Within myself a process of
organization or interpenetration of conscious
states is going on, which constitutes true duration.
It is because I *endure* in this way that I picture
to myself what I call the past oscillations of the
pendulum at the same time as I perceive the
present oscillation. Now, let us withdraw for a
moment the ego which thinks these so-called successive oscillations : there will never be more
than a single oscillation, and indeed only a single
position, of the pendulum, and hence no duration.
Withdraw, on the other hand, the pendulum and
its oscillations ; there will no longer be anything
but the heterogeneous duration of the ego,
without moments external to one another, without relation to number. Thus, within our ego,
there is succession without mutual externality ;
outside the ego, in pure space, mutual externality
without succession : mutual externality, since
the present oscillation is radically distinct from
the previous oscillation, which no longer exists ;
but no succession, since succession exists solely
for a conscious spectator who keeps the past in

But what we call measuring time is nothing but counting simultaneities. The clock taken as an illustration.

mind and sets the two oscillations or their symbols side by side in an auxiliary space. Now,
between this succession without externality and
this externality without succession, a kind of
exchange takes place, very similar to what physicists call the phenomenon of endosmosis. As the
successive phases of our conscious life, although
interpenetrating, correspond individually to an
oscillation of the pendulum which occurs at the
same time, and as, moreover, these oscillations
are sharply distinguished from one another, we
get into the habit of setting up the same distinction between the successive moments of our conscious life : the oscillations of the pendulum
break it up, so to speak, into parts external to
one another : hence the mistaken idea of a homogeneous inner duration, similar to space, the
moments of which are identical and follow, without penetrating, one another. But, on the other
hand, the oscillations of the pendulum, which
are distinct only because one has disappeared
when the other appears on the scene, profit, as
it were, from the influence which they have thus
exercised over our conscious life. Owing to the
fact that our consciousness has organized them
as a whole in memory, they are first preserved
and afterwards disposed in a series : in a word,
we create for them a fourth dimension of space,
which we call homogeneous time, and which
enables the movement of the pendulum, although
taking place at one spot, to be continually set in

juxtaposition to itself. Now, if we try to determine the exact part played by the real and the
imaginary in this very complex process, this is
what we find. There is a real space, without
duration, in which phenomena appear and disappear simultaneously with our states of consciousness. There is a real duration, the heterogeneous
moments of which permeate one another ; each
moment, however, can be brought into relation with
a state of the external world which is contemporaneous with it, and can be separated from the
other moments in consequence of this very process. The comparison of these two realities gives
rise to a symbolical representation of duration,
derived from space. Duration thus assumes the
illusory form of a homogeneous medium, and
the connecting link between these two terms, space
and duration, is simultaneity, which might be
defined as the intersection of time and space.

If we analyse in the same way the concept of
motion, the living symbol of this seemingly homogeneous duration, we shall be led to
make a distinction of the same kind.
We generally say that a movement
takes place *in* space, and when we assert
that motion is homogeneous and divisible, it is of the space traversed that
we are thinking, as if it were inter-
changeable with the motion itself. Now, if we
reflect further, we shall see that the successive
positions of the moving body really do occupy

*Two elements
in motion : (1)
the space tra-
versed, which
is homogene-
ous and divi-
sible ; (2) the
act of travers-
ing, indivisi-
ble and real
only for con-
sciousness.*

space, but that the process by which it passes
from one position to the other, a process which
occupies duration and which has no reality except for a conscious spectator, eludes space. We
have to do here not with an *object* but with a
progress : motion, in so far as it is a passage from
one point to another, is a mental synthesis, a
psychic and therefore unextended process. Space
contains only parts of space, and at whatever point
of space we consider the moving body, we shall
get only a position. If consciousness is aware
of anything more than positions, the reason is
that it keeps the successive positions in mind and
synthesizes them. But how does it carry out a
synthesis of this kind ? It cannot be by a fresh
setting out of these same positions in a homogeneous medium, for a fresh synthesis would be
necessary to connect the positions with one
another, and so on indefinitely. We are thus compelled to admit that we have here to do with a
synthesis which is, so to speak, qualitative, a
gradual organization of our successive sensations,
a unity resembling that of a phrase in a melody.
This is just the idea of motion which we form
when we think of it by itself, when, so to speak,
from motion we extract mobility. Think of
what you experience on suddenly perceiving a
shooting star : in this extremely rapid motion
there is a natural and instinctive separation between the space traversed, which appears to you
under the form of a line of fire, and the absolutely

indivisible sensation of motion or mobility. A rapid gesture, made with one's eyes shut, will assume for consciousness the form of a purely qualitative sensation as long as there is no thought of the space traversed. In a word, there are two elements to be distinguished in motion, the space traversed and the act by which we traverse it, the successive positions and the synthesis of these positions. The first of these elements is a homogeneous quantity : the second has no reality except in a consciousness : it is a quality or an intensity, whichever you prefer. But here again we meet with a case of endosmosis, an inter-mingling of the purely intensive sensation of mobility with the extensive representation of the space traversed. On the one hand we attribute to the motion the divisibility of the space which it traverses, forgetting that it is quite possible to divide an *object*, but not an *act* : and on the other hand we accustom ourselves to projecting this act itself into space, to applying it to the whole of the line which the moving body traverses, in a word, to solidifying it : as if this localizing of a *progress* in space did not amount to asserting that, even outside consciousness, the past co-exists along with the present !

It is to this confusion between motion and the space traversed that the paradoxes of the Eleatics are due ; for the interval which separates two points is infinitely divisible, and if motion con-sisted of parts like those of the interval itself,

the interval would never be crossed. But the
truth is that each of Achilles' steps is
a simple indivisible act, and that, after
a given number of these acts, Achilles
will have passed the tortoise. The mistake of the Eleatics arises from their
identification of this series of acts, each of which is
of a definite kind and *indivisible*, with the homogeneous space which underlies them. As this
space can be divided and put together again according to any law whatever, they think they are
justified in reconstructing Achilles' whole movement, not with Achilles' kind of step, but with the
tortoise's kind : in place of Achilles pursuing the
tortoise they really put two tortoises, regulated
by each other, two tortoises which agree to make
the same kind of steps or simultaneous acts, so as
never to catch one another.   Why does Achilles
outstrip the tortoise ?   Because each of Achilles'
steps and each of the tortoise's steps are indivisible
acts in so far as they are movements, and are
different magnitudes in so far as they are space :
so that addition will soon give a greater length
for the space traversed by Achilles than is obtained
by adding together the space traversed by the
tortoise and the handicap with which it started.
This is what Zeno leaves out of account when he
reconstructs the movement of Achilles according
to the same law as the movement of the tortoise,
forgetting that space alone can be divided and
put together again in any way we like, and thus

The common confusion between motion and the space traversed gives rise to the paradoxes of the Eleatics.

I

confusing space with motion.   Hence we do not
think it necessary to admit, even after the acute
and profound analysis of a contemporary thinker,[1]
that the meeting of the two moving bodies
implies a discrepancy between real and imaginary
motion, between *space in itself* and indefinitely
divisible space, between concrete time and abstract
time.   Why resort to a metaphysical hypothesis,
however ingenious, about the nature of space,
time, and motion, when immediate intuition shows
us motion within duration, and duration outside
space ?   There is no need to assume a limit to
the divisibility of concrete space ; we can admit
that it is infinitely divisible, provided that we
make a distinction between the simultaneous
positions of the two moving bodies, which are in
fact in space, and their movements, which cannot
occupy space, being duration rather than extent,
quality and not quantity.   To measure the velocity of a movement, as we shall see, is simply to
ascertain a simultaneity ; to introduce this velocity into calculations is simply to use a convenient
means of anticipating a simultaneity.   Thus mathematics confines itself to its own province as long
as it is occupied with determining the simultaneous positions of Achilles and the tortoise at a
given moment, or when it admits *a priori* that
the two moving bodies meet at a point X—a
meeting which is itself a simultaneity.   But it goes

[1] Evellin, *Infini et quantité*.   Paris, 1881.

beyond its province when it claims to reconstruct what takes place in the interval between two simultaneities ; or rather it is inevitably led, even then, to consider simultaneities once more, fresh simultaneities, the indefinitely increasing number of which ought to be a warning that we cannot make movement out of immobilities, nor time out of space. In short, just as nothing will be found homogeneous in duration except a symbolical medium with no duration at all, namely space, in which simultaneities are set out in line, in the same way no homogeneous element will be found in motion except that which least belongs to it, the traversed space, which is motionless.

Now, just for this reason, science cannot deal with time and motion except on condition of first **Science has to** eliminating the essential and qualita- **eliminate dur-** tive element—of time, duration, and of **ation from** **time and mo-** motion, mobility. We may easily con- **bility from** **motion before** vince ourselves of this by examining the **it can deal** **with them.** part played in astronomy and mechanics by considerations of time, motion, and velocity.

Treatises on mechanics are careful to announce that they do not intend to define duration itself but only the equality of two durations. " Two intervals of time are equal when two identical bodies, in identical conditions at the beginning of each of these intervals and subject to the same actions and influences of every kind, have traversed the same space at the end of these intervals." In other words, we are to note the exact moment at which the motion begins, i.e. the coincidence of an external change with one of our psychic states ; we are to note the moment at which the motion ends, that is to say, another simultaneity ; finally we are to measure the space traversed, the only thing, in fact, which is really measurable.   Hence there is no question here of duration, but only of space and simultaneities.   To announce that something will take place at the end of a time t is to declare that consciousness will note between now and then a number t of simultaneities of a certain kind.   And we must not be led astray by the words " between now and then," for the interval of duration exists only for us and on account of the interpenetration of our conscious states. Outside ourselves we should find only space, and consequently nothing but simultaneities, of which we could not even say that they are objectively successive, since succession can only be thought through *comparing* the present with the past.—That the interval of duration itself cannot be taken into account by science is proved by the fact that, if all the motions of the universe took place twice or thrice as quickly, there would be nothing to alter either in our formulae or in the figures which are to be found in them.   Consciousness would have an indefinable and as it were qualitative impression of the change, but the change would not make itself felt outside consciousness, since the same number of simultaneities would go on taking place in space.   We shall see, later on, that when the astronomer predicts, e.g., an eclipse, he does something of this kind : he shortens infinitely the intervals of duration, as these do not count for science, and thus perceives in a very short time—a few seconds at the most—a succession of simultaneities which may take up several centuries for the concrete consciousness, compelled to live through the intervals instead of merely counting their extremities.

A direct analysis of the notion of velocity will bring us to the same conclusion.   Mechanics gets

This is seen in the definition of velocity. this notion through a series of ideas, the connexion of which it is easy enough to trace.   It first builds up the idea of uniform motion by picturing, on the one hand, the path AB of a certain moving body, and, on the other, a physical phenomenon which is repeated indefinitely under the same conditions, e.g., a stone always falling from the same height on to the same spot.   If we mark on the path AB the points M, N, P . . . reached by the moving body at each of the moments when the stone touches the ground, and if the intervals AM, MN and NP are found to be equal to one another, the motion will be said to be uniform : and any one of these intervals will be called the velocity of the moving body, provided that it is agreed to adopt as unit of duration the physical phenomenon which has been chosen as the term of comparison.   Thus, the velocity of a uniform motion is defined by mechanics without appealing to any other notions

than those of space and simultaneity. Now let us
turn to the case of a variable motion, that is, to the
case when the elements AM, MN, NP . . . are
found to be unequal. In order to define the
velocity of the moving body A at the point M, we
shall only have to imagine an unlimited number of
moving bodies A_1, A_2, A_3 . . . all moving uni-
formly with velocities v_1, v_2, v_3 . . . which are
arranged, e.g., in an ascending scale and which
correspond to all possible magnitudes. Let us
then consider on the path of the moving body A
two points M' and M", situated on either side of
the point M but very near it. At the same time
as this moving body reaches the points M', M, M",
the other moving bodies reach points $M'_1 M_1 M''_1$,
$M'_2 M_2 M''_2$ . . . on their respective paths ; and
there must be two moving bodies A_h and A_p such
that we have on the one hand M' M = M'_h M_h and
on the other hand MM" = M_p M''_p. We shall then
agree to say that the velocity of the moving body
A at the point M lies between v_h and v_p. But
nothing prevents our assuming that the points
M' and M" are still nearer the point M, and it will
then be necessary to replace v_h and v_p by two
fresh velocities v_l and v_n, the one greater than
v_h and the other less than v_p. And in proportion
as we reduce the two intervals M'M and MM", we
shall lessen the difference between the velocities
of the uniform corresponding movements. Now,
the two intervals being capable of decreasing right
down to zero, there evidently exists between v_l

and v_n a certain velocity v_m, such that the difference between this velocity and v_h, v_l . . . on the
one hand, and v_p, v_n . . . on the other, can become smaller than any given quantity.   It is this
common limit v_m which we shall call the velocity
of the moving body A at the point M.—Now, in
this analysis of variable motion, as in that of
uniform motion, it is a question only of spaces once
traversed and of simultaneous positions once
reached.   We were thus justified in saying that,
while all that mechanics retains of time is simultaneity, all that it retains of motion itself—
restricted, as it is, to a *measurement* of motion—
is immobility.

This result might have been foreseen by noticing
that mechanics necessarily deals with equations,

Mechanics deals with equations, which express something finished, and not processes, such as duration and motion.

and that an algebraic equation always
expresses something already done.   Now,
it is of the very essence of duration and
motion, as they appear to our consciousness, to be something that is unceasingly
being done ; thus algebra can represent
the results gained at a certain moment of duration
and the positions occupied by a certain moving
body in space, but not duration and motion themselves.   Mathematics may, indeed, increase the
number of simultaneities and positions which it
takes into consideration by making the intervals
very small : it may even, by using the differential
instead of the difference, show that it is possible
to increase without limit the number of these

intervals of duration. Nevertheless, however small the interval is supposed to be, it is the extremity of the interval at which mathematics always places itself. As for the interval itself, as for the duration and the motion, they are necessarily left out of the equation. The reason is that duration and motion are mental syntheses, and not objects ; that, although the moving body occupies, one after the other, points on a line, motion itself has nothing to do with a line ; and finally that, although the positions occupied by the moving body vary with the different moments of duration, though it even creates distinct moments by the mere fact of occupying different positions, duration properly so called has no moments which are identical or external to one another, being essentially heterogeneous, continuous, and with no analogy to number.

It follows from this analysis that space alone is homogeneous, that objects in space form a discrete multiplicity, and that every discrete multiplicity is got by a process of unfolding in space. It also follows that there is neither duration nor even succession in space, if we give to these words the meaning in which consciousness takes them : each of the so-called successive states of the external world exists alone ; their multiplicity is real only for a consciousness that can first retain them and then set them side by side by externalizing them in relation

Conclusion : space alone is homogeneous : duration and succession belong not to the external world, but to the conscious mind.

to one another. If it retains them, it is because
these distinct states of the external world give rise
to states of consciousness which permeate one
another, imperceptibly organize themselves into
a whole, and bind the past to the present by
this very process of connexion. If it externalizes
them in relation to one another, the reason is that,
thinking of their radical distinctness (the one
having ceased to be when the other appears on the
scene), it perceives them under the form of a discrete
multiplicity, which amounts to setting them out in
line, in the space in which each of them existed
separately. The space employed for this purpose
is just that which is called homogeneous time.

But another conclusion results from this analysis,
namely, that the multiplicity of conscious states,

Two kinds of
multiplicity :
two senses of
the word "dis-
tinguish," the
one qualita-
tive and the
other quanti-
tative. regarded in its original purity, is not at
all like the discrete multiplicity which
goes to form a number. In such a case
there is, as we said, a qualitative multiplicity. In short, we must admit two
kinds of multiplicity, two possible senses
of the word " distinguish," two conceptions, the
one qualitative and the other quantitative, of the
difference between *same* and *other*. Sometimes
this multiplicity, this distinctness, this heterogeneity contains number only potentially, as
Aristotle would have said. Consciousness, then,
makes a qualitative discrimination without any
further thought of counting the qualities or
even of distinguishing them as *several*. In such

a case we have multiplicity without quantity. Sometimes, on the other hand, it is a question of a multiplicity of terms which are counted or which are conceived as capable of being counted ; but we think then of the possibility of externalizing them in relation to one another, we set them out in space. Unfortunately, we are so accustomed to illustrate one of these two meanings of the same word by the other, and even to perceive the one in the other, that we find it extraordinarily difficult to distinguish between them or at least to express this distinction in words. Thus I said that several conscious states are organized into a whole, permeate one another, gradually gain a richer content, and might thus give any one ignorant of space the feeling of pure duration; but the very use of the word " several " shows that I had already isolated these states, externalized them in relation to one another, and, in a word, set them side by side ; thus, by the very language which I was compelled to use, I betrayed the deeply ingrained habit of setting out time in space. From this spatial setting out, already accomplished, we are compelled to borrow the terms which we use to describe the state of a mind which has not yet accomplished it : these terms are thus misleading from the very beginning, and the idea of a multiplicity without relation to number or space, although clear for pure reflective thought, cannot be translated into the language of common sense. And yet we cannot even form the idea of discrete multiplicity without considering at the same time a qualitative multiplicity. When we explicitly count units by stringing them along a spatial line, is it not the case that, alongside this addition of identical terms standing out from a homogeneous background, an organization of these units is going on in the depths of the soul, a wholly dynamic process, not unlike the purely qualitative way in which an anvil, if it could feel, would realize a series of blows from a hammer? In this sense we might almost say that the numbers in daily use have each their emotional equivalent. Tradesmen are well aware of it, and instead of indicating the price of an object by a round number of shillings, they will mark the next smaller number, leaving themselves to insert afterwards a sufficient number of pence and farthings. In a word, the process by which we count units and make them into a discrete multiplicity has two sides; on the one hand we assume that they are identical, which is conceivable only on condition that these units are ranged alongside each other in a homogeneous medium; but on the other hand the third unit, for example, when added to the other two, alters the nature, the appearance and, as it were, the rhythm of the whole; without this interpenetration and this, so to speak, qualitative progress, no addition would be possible. Hence it is through the quality of quantity that we form the idea of quantity without quality.

It is therefore obvious that, if it did not betake itself to a symbolical substitute, our consciousness would never regard time as a homogeneous medium, in which the terms of a succession remain outside one another. But we naturally reach this symbolical representation by the mere fact that, in a series of identical terms, each term

Our successive sensations are regarded as mutually external, like their objective causes, and this reacts on our deeper psychic life.

assumes a double aspect for our consciousness : one aspect which is the same for all of them, since we are thinking then of the sameness of the external object, and another aspect which is characteristic of each of them, because the supervening of each term brings about a new organization of the whole. Hence the possibility of setting out in space, under the form of numerical multiplicity, what we have called a qualitative multiplicity, and of regarding the one as the equivalent of the other. Now, this twofold process is nowhere accomplished so easily as in the perception of the external phenomenon which takes for us the form of motion. Here we certainly have a series of identical terms, since it is always the same moving body ; but, on the other hand, the synthesis carried out by our consciousness between the actual position and what our memory calls the former positions, causes these images to permeate, complete, and, so to speak, continue one another. Hence, it is principally by the help of motion that duration assumes the form of a homogeneous medium, and that time is projected into space. But, even if we leave out motion, any repetition of a well-marked external phenomenon would suggest to consciousness the same mode of representation. Thus, when we hear a series of blows of a hammer, the sounds form an indivisible melody in so far as they are pure sensations, and, here again, give rise to a dynamic progress ; but, knowing that the same objective cause is at work, we cut up this progress into phases which we then regard as identical ; and this multiplicity of elements no longer being conceivable except by being set out in space, since they have now become identical, we are necessarily led to the idea of a homogeneous time, the symbolical image of real duration. In a word, our ego comes in contact with the external world at its surface ; our successive sensations, although dissolving into one another, retain something of the mutual externality which belongs to their objective causes ; and thus our superficial psychic life comes to be pictured without any great effort as set out in a homogeneous medium. But the symbolical character of such a picture becomes more striking as we advance further into the depths of consciousness : the deep-seated self which ponders and decides, which heats and blazes up, is a self whose states and changes permeate one another and undergo a deep alteration as soon as we separate them from one another in order to set them out in space. But as this deeper self forms one and the same person with the superficial ego, the two seem to *endure* in the same way. And as the repeated picture of one identical objective phenomenon, ever recurring, cuts up our superficial psychic life into parts external to one another, the moments which are thus determined determine in their turn distinct segments in the dynamic and undivided progress of our more personal conscious states. Thus the mutual externality which material objects gain from their juxtaposition in homogeneous space reverberates and spreads into the depths of consciousness : little by little our sensations are distinguished from one another like the external causes which gave rise to them, and our feelings or ideas come to be separated like the sensations with which they are contemporaneous.

That our ordinary conception of duration depends on a gradual incursion of space into the domain of pure consciousness is proved by the fact that, in order to deprive the ego of the faculty of perceiving a homogeneous time, it is enough to take away from it this outer circle of psychic states which it uses as a balance-wheel. These conditions are realized when we dream ; for sleep, by relaxing the play of the organic functions, alters the communicating surface between the ego and external objects. Here we no longer measure duration, but we feel it ; from quantity it returns to the state of quality ; we no longer estimate past time mathematically : the mathematical estimate gives place to a confused instinct,

Eliminate the superficial psychic states, and we no longer perceive a homogeneous time or measure duration, but feel it as a quality.

capable, like all instincts, of committing gross
errors, but also of acting at times with extraordinary skill.   Even in the waking state, daily experience ought to teach us to distinguish between
duration as quality, that which consciousness
reaches immediately and which is probably what
animals perceive, and time so to speak materialized,
time that has become quantity by being set out in
space.   Whilst I am writing these lines, the hour
strikes on a neighbouring clock, but my inatten-
tive ear does not perceive it until several strokes
have made themselves heard.   Hence I have not
counted them ; and yet I only have to turn my
attention backwards to count up the four strokes
which have already sounded and add them to
those which I hear.   If, then, I question myself
carefully on what has just taken place, I perceive
that the first four sounds had struck my ear and
even affected my consciousness, but that the sensations produced by each one of them, instead of
being set side by side, had melted into one another
in such a way as to give the whole a peculiar quality,
to make a kind of musical phrase out of it.   In
order, then, to estimate retrospectively the number
of strokes sounded, I tried to reconstruct this phrase
in thought : my imagination made one stroke, then
two, then three, and as long as it did not reach the
exact number four, my feeling, when consulted,
answered that the total effect was qualitatively
different.   It had thus ascertained in its own
way the succession of four strokes, but quite other-

wise than by a process of addition, and without bringing in the image of a juxtaposition of distinct terms. In a word, the number of strokes was perceived as a quality and not as a quantity : it is thus that duration is presented to immediate consciousness, and it retains this form so long as it does not give place to a symbolical representation derived from extensity.

We should therefore distinguish two forms of multiplicity, two very different ways of regarding duration, two aspects of conscious life. Below homogeneous duration, which is the extensive symbol of true duration, a close psychological analysis distinguishes a duration whose heterogeneous moments permeate one another ; below the numerical multiplicity of conscious states, a qualitative multiplicity ; below the self with well-defined states, a self in which *succeeding each other* means *melting into one another* and forming an organic whole. But we are generally content with the first, i.e. with the shadow of the self projected into homogeneous space. Consciousness, goaded by an insatiable desire to separate, substitutes the symbol for the reality, or perceives the reality only through the symbol. As the self thus refracted, and thereby broken to pieces, is much better adapted to the requirements of social life in general and language in particular, consciousness prefers it, and gradually loses sight of the fundamental self.

There are therefore two forms of multiplicity, of duration and conscious life.

In order to recover this fundamental self, as the unsophisticated consciousness would perceive it, a vigorous effort of analysis is necessary, which will isolate the fluid inner states from their image, first refracted, then solidified in homogeneous space. In other words, our perceptions, sensations, emotions and ideas occur under two aspects : the one clear and precise, but impersonal; the other confused, ever changing, and inexpressible, because language cannot get hold of it without arresting its mobility or fit it into its common-place forms without making it into public property. If we have been led to distinguish two forms of multiplicity, two forms of duration, we must expect each conscious state, taken by itself, to assume a different aspect according as we consider it within a discrete multiplicity or a confused multiplicity, in the time as quality, in which it is produced, or in the time as quantity, into which it is projected.

When e.g. I take my first walk in a town in which I am going to live, my environment produces on me two impressions at the same time, one of which is destined to last while the other will constantly change. Every day I perceive the same houses, and as I know that they are the same objects, I always call them by the same name and I also fancy that they always look the same to me. But if I recur, at the end of a sufficiently long period, to the impression

The two aspects of our conscious states.

One of which is due to the solidifying influence of external objects and language on our constantly changing feelings.

K

which I experienced during the first few years,
I am surprised at the remarkable, inexplicable,
and indeed inexpressible change which has taken
place. It seems that these objects, continually
perceived by me and constantly impressing themselves on my mind, have ended by borrowing
from me something of my own conscious existence ;
like myself they have lived, and like myself they
have grown old. This is not a mere illusion ;
for if to-day's impression were absolutely identical
with that of yesterday, what difference would
there be between perceiving and recognizing,
between learning and remembering ? Yet this
difference escapes the attention of most of us ; we
shall hardly perceive it, unless we are warned of
it and then carefully look into ourselves. The
reason is that our outer and, so to speak, social
life is more practically important to us than our
inner and individual existence. We instinctively
tend to solidify our impressions in order to express
them in language. Hence we confuse the feeling
itself, which is in a perpetual state of becoming,
with its permanent external object, and especially
with the word which expresses this object. In
the same way as the fleeting duration of our ego
is fixed by its projection in homogeneous space,
our constantly changing impressions, wrapping
themselves round the external object which is
their cause, take on its definite outlines and its
immobility.

Our simple sensations, taken in their natural

state, are still more fleeting. Such and such a
flavour, such and such a scent, pleased
me when I was a child though I dislike
them to-day. Yet I still give the same
name to the sensation experienced, and
I speak as if only my taste had changed, whilst the
scent and the flavour have remained the same.
Thus I again solidify the sensation ; and when
its changeableness becomes so obvious that I cannot
help recognizing it, I abstract this changeableness
to give it a name of its own and solidify it in the
shape of a *taste*. But in reality there are neither
identical sensations nor multiple tastes : for
sensations and tastes seem to me to be *objects* as
soon as I isolate and name them, and in the
human soul there are only *processes*. What I
ought to say is that every sensation is altered by
repetition, and that if it does not seem to me to
change from day to day, it is because I perceive
it through the object which is its cause, through
the word which translates it. This influence of
language on sensation is deeper than is usually
thought. Not only does language make us believe
in the unchangeableness of our sensations, but it
will sometimes deceive us as to the nature of the
sensation felt. Thus, when I partake of a dish
that is supposed to be exquisite, the name which
it bears, suggestive of the approval given to it,
comes between my sensation and my consciousness;
I may believe that the flavour pleases me when a
slight effort of attention would prove the contrary.

How language gives a fixed form to fleeting sensations.

(P²)

In short, the word with well-defined outlines, the rough and ready word, which stores up the stable, common, and consequently impersonal element in the impressions of mankind, overwhelms or at least covers over the delicate and fugitive impressions of our individual consciousness. To maintain the struggle on equal terms, the latter ought to express themselves in precise words ; but these words, as soon as they were formed, would turn against the sensation which gave birth to them, and, invented to show that the sensation is unstable, they would impose on it their own stability.

This overwhelming of the immediate consciousness is nowhere so striking as in the case of our **How analysis** feelings. A violent love or a deep **and descrip-** melancholy takes possession of our **tion distort** **the feelings.** soul : here we feel a thousand different elements which dissolve into and permeate one another without any precise outlines, without the least tendency to externalize themselves in relation to one another ; hence their originality. We distort them as soon as we distinguish a numerical multiplicity in their confused mass : what will it be, then, when we set them out, isolated from one another, in this homogeneous medium which may be called either time or space, whichever you prefer ? A moment ago each of them was borrowing an indefinable colour from its surroundings : now we have it colourless, and ready to accept a name. The feeling itself is a being which lives and develops and is therefore constantly changing ; otherwise how could it gradually lead us to form a resolution ? Our resolution would be immediately taken. But it lives because the duration in which it develops is a duration whose moments permeate one another. By separating these moments from each other, by spreading out time in space, we have caused this feeling to lose its life and its colour. Hence, we are now standing before our own shadow : we believe that we have analysed our feeling, while we have really replaced it by a juxtaposition of lifeless states which can be translated into words, and each of which constitutes the common element, the impersonal residue, of the impressions felt in a given case by the whole of society. And this is why we reason about these states and apply our simple logic to them : having set them up as genera by the mere fact of having isolated them from one another, we have prepared them for use in some future deduction. Now, if some bold novelist, tearing aside the cleverly woven curtain of our conventional ego, shows us under this appearance of logic a fundamental absurdity, under this juxtaposition of simple states an infinite permeation of a thousand different impressions which have already ceased to exist the instant they are named, we commend him for having known us better than we knew ourselves. This is not the case, however, and the very fact that he spreads out our feeling in a homogeneous

time, and expresses its elements by words, shows
that he in his turn is only offering us its shadow :
but he has arranged this shadow in such a way as
to make us suspect the extraordinary and illogical
nature of the object which projects it ; he has
made us reflect by giving outward expression to
something of that contradiction, that interpenetration, which is the very essence of the elements
expressed. Encouraged by him, we have put
aside for an instant the veil which we interposed
between our consciousness and ourselves. He
has brought us back into our own presence.

We should experience the same sort of surprise
if we strove to seize our ideas themselves in their
natural state, as our consciousness would
perceive them if it were no longer beset
by space. This breaking up of the
constituent elements of an idea, which
issues in abstraction, is too convenient
for us to do without it in ordinary life
and even in philosophical discussion. But when
we fancy that the parts thus artificially separated are the genuine threads with which the
concrete idea was woven, when, substituting for
the interpenetration of the real terms the juxtaposition of their symbols, we claim to make
duration out of space, we unavoidably fall into the
mistakes of associationism. We shall not insist
on the latter point, which will be the subject of a
thorough examination in the next chapter. Let
it be enough to say that the impulsive zeal with

On the sur-
face our con-
scious states
obey the laws
of association.
Deeper down
they interpene-
trate and
form a part of
ourselves.

which we take sides on certain questions shows how
our intellect has its instincts—and what can an
instinct of this kind be if not an impetus common
to all our ideas, i.e. their very interpenetration ?
The beliefs to which we most strongly adhere are
those of which we should find it most difficult to
give an account, and the reasons by which we
justify them are seldom those which have led us to
adopt them.   In a certain sense we have adopted
them without any reason, for what makes them
valuable in our eyes is that they match the colour
of all our other ideas, and that from the very
first we have seen in them something of ourselves.
Hence they do not take in our minds that common
looking form which they will assume as soon as we
try to give expression to them in words ; and,
although they bear the same name in other minds,
they are by no means the same thing.   The fact
is that each of them has the same kind of life as a
cell in an organism : everything which affects the
general state of the self affects it also.   But while
the cell occupies a definite point in the organism,
an idea which is truly ours fills the whole of our
self.   Not all our ideas, however, are thus incorporated in the fluid mass of our conscious states.
Many float on the surface, like dead leaves on the
water of a pond : the mind, when it thinks
them over and over again, finds them ever the
same, as if they were external to it. Among
these are the ideas which we receive ready made,
and which remain in us without ever being

properly assimilated, or again the ideas which we have omitted to cherish and which have withered in neglect. If, in proportion as we get away from the deeper strata of the self, our conscious states tend more and more to assume the form of a numerical multiplicity, and to spread out in a homogeneous space, it is just because these conscious states tend to become more and more lifeless, more and more impersonal. Hence we need not be surprised if only those ideas which least belong to us can be adequately expressed in words : only to these, as we shall see, does the associationist theory apply. External to one another, they keep up relations among themselves in which the inmost nature of each of them counts for nothing, relations which can therefore be classified. It may thus be said that they are associated by contiguity or for some logical reason. But if, digging below the surface of contact between the self and external objects, we penetrate into the depths of the organized and living intelligence, we shall witness the joining together or rather the blending of many ideas which, when once dissociated, seem to exclude one another as logically contradictory terms. The strangest dreams, in which two images overlie one another and show us at the same time two different persons, who yet make only one, will hardly give us an idea of the interweaving of concepts which goes on when we are awake. The imagination of the dreamer, cut off from the external world, imitates with mere images, and parodies in its own way, the process which constantly goes on with regard to ideas in the deeper regions of the intellectual life.

Thus may be verified, thus, too, will be illustrated by a further study of deep-seated psychic phenomena the principle from which

By separating our conscious states we promote social life, but raise problems soluble only by recourse to the concrete and living self. we started : conscious life displays two aspects according as we perceive it directly or by refraction through space. Considered in themselves, the deep-seated conscious states have no relation to quantity, they are pure quality ; they intermingle in such a way that we cannot tell whether they are one or several, nor even examine them from this point of view without at once altering their nature. The duration which they thus create is a duration whose moments do not constitute a numerical multiplicity : to characterize these moments by saying that they encroach on one another would still be to distinguish them. If each of us lived a purely individual life, if there were neither society nor language, would our consciousness grasp the series of inner states in this unbroken form ? Undoubtedly it would not quite succeed, because we should still retain the idea of a homogeneous space in which objects are sharply distinguished from one another, and because it is too convenient to set out in such a medium the somewhat cloudy states which first attract the attention of consciousness, in order to resolve them into simpler terms. But mark that the intuition of a homogeneous space is already a step towards social life. Probably animals do not picture to themselves, beside their sensations, as we do, an external world quite distinct from themselves, which is the common property of all conscious beings. Our tendency to form a clear picture of this externality of things and the homogeneity of their medium is the same as the impulse which leads us to live in common and to speak. But, in proportion as the conditions of social life are more completely realized, the current which carries our conscious states from within outwards is strengthened ; little by little these states are made into objects or things ; they break off not only from one another, but from ourselves. Henceforth we no longer perceive them except in the homogeneous medium in which we have set their image, and through the word which lends them its commonplace colour. Thus a second self is formed which obscures the first, a self whose existence is made up of distinct moments, whose states are separated from one another and easily expressed in words. I do not mean, here, to split up the personality, nor to bring back in another form the numerical multiplicity which I shut out at the beginning. It is the same self which perceives distinct states at first, and which, by afterwards concentrating its attention, will see these states melt into one another like the crystals of a snow-flake when touched

for some time with the finger.   And, in truth, for
the sake of language, the self has everything to
gain by not bringing back confusion where order
reigns, and in not upsetting this ingenious arrangement of almost impersonal states by which it has
ceased to form " a kingdom within a kingdom."
An inner life with well distinguished moments
and with clearly characterized states will answer
better the requirements of social life.   Indeed, a
superficial psychology may be content with de-
scribing it without thereby falling into error, on
condition, however, that it restricts itself to the
study of what has taken place and leaves out what
is going on.   But if, passing from statics to dynam-
ics, this psychology claims to reason about
things in the making as it reasoned about things
made, if it offers us the concrete and living self as
an association of terms which are distinct from
one another and are set side by side in a homogeneous medium, it will see difficulty after difficulty rising in its path.   And these difficulties
will multiply the greater the efforts it makes to
overcome them, for all its efforts will only bring
into clearer light the absurdity of the fundamental
hypothesis by which it spreads out time in space and
puts succession at the very centre of simultaneity.
We shall see that the contradictions implied in the
problems of causality, freedom, personality, spring
from no other source, and that, if we wish to get
rid of them, we have only to go back to the real and
concrete self and give up its symbolical substitute.

CHAPTER III

THE ORGANIZATION OF CONSCIOUS STATES
FREE WILL

IT is easy to see why the question of free will brings into conflict these two rival systems of nature, mechanism and dynamism. Dynamism starts from the idea of voluntary activity, given by consciousness, and comes to represent inertia by gradually emptying this idea : it has thus no difficulty in conceiving free force on the one hand and matter governed by laws on the other. Mechanism follows the opposite course. It assumes that the materials which it synthesizes are governed by necessary laws, and although it reaches richer and richer combinations, which are more and more difficult to foresee, and to all appearance more and more contingent, yet it never gets out of the narrow circle of necessity within which it at first shut itself up.

Mechanism, dynamism, and free will.

A thorough examination of these two conceptions of nature will show that they involve two very different hypotheses as to the relations between laws and the facts which they govern. As he looks higher and higher, the believer in dynamism thinks that he perceives facts which more and more elude the grasp of laws : he thus

For dynamism facts more real than laws : mechanism reverses this attitude. The idea of spontaneity simpler than that of inertia.

sets up the fact as the absolute reality, and the law as the more or less symbolical expression of this reality. Mechanism, on the contrary, discovers within the particular fact a certain number of laws of which the fact is thus made to be the meeting point, and nothing else : on this hypothesis it is the law which becomes the genuine reality. Now, if it is asked why the one party assigns a higher reality to the fact and the other to the law, it will be found that mechanism and dynamism take the word *simplicity* in two very different senses. For the first, any principle is simple of which the effects can be foreseen and even calculated : thus, by the very definition, the notion of inertia becomes simpler than that of freedom, the homogeneous simpler than the heterogeneous, the abstract simpler than the concrete. But dynamism is not anxious so much to arrange the notions in the most convenient order as to find out their real relationship : often, in fact, the so-called simple notion—that which the believer in mechanism regards as primitive—has been obtained by the blending together of several richer notions which seem to be derived from it, and which have more or less neutralized one another in this very process of blending, just as darkness may be produced by the interference of two lights. Regarded from this new point of view, the idea of spontaneity is indisputably simpler than that of inertia, since the second can be understood and defined only by means of the first, while the first is self-sufficient. For each of us has the immediate knowledge (be it thought true or fallacious) of his free spontaneity, without the notion of inertia having anything to do with this knowledge. But, if we wish to define the inertia of matter, we must say that it cannot move or stop of its own accord, that every body perseveres in the state of rest or motion so long as it is not acted upon by any force : and in both cases we are unavoidably carried back to the idea of activity. It is therefore natural that, *a priori*, we should reach two opposite conceptions of human activity, according to the way in which we understand the relation between the concrete and the abstract, the simple and the complex, facts and laws.

A posteriori, however, definite facts are appealed to against freedom, some physical, others psychological. Sometimes it is asserted that our actions are necessitated by our feelings, our ideas, and the whole preceding series of our conscious states ; sometimes freedom is denounced as being incompatible with the fundamental properties of matter, and in particular with the principle of the conservation of energy. Hence two kinds of determinism, two apparently different empirical proofs of universal necessity. We shall show that the second of these two forms is reducible to the first, and that all determinism, even physical determinism, involves a psychological hypothesis : we shall then prove

Determinism : (1) physical (2) psychological. Former reducible to latter, which itself rests on inaccurate conception of multiplicity of conscious states or duration.

that psychological determinism itself, and the refutations which are given of it, rest on an inaccurate conception of the multiplicity of conscious states, or rather of duration. Thus, in the light of the principles worked out in the foregoing chapter, we shall see a self emerge whose activity cannot be compared to that of any other force.

Physical determinism, in its latest form, is closely bound up with mechanical or rather kinetic theories of matter. The universe is pictured as a heap of matter which the imagination resolves into molecules and atoms. These particles are supposed to carry out unceasingly movements of every kind, sometimes of vibration, sometimes of translation ; and physical phenomena, chemical action, the qualities of matter which our senses perceive, heat, sound, electricity, perhaps even attraction, are thought to be reducible objectively to these elementary movements. The matter which goes to make up organized bodies being subject to the same laws, we find in the nervous system, for example, only molecules and atoms which are in motion and attract and repel one another. Now if all bodies, organized or unorganized, thus act and react on one another in their ultimate parts, it is obvious that the molecular state of the brain at a given moment will be modified by the shocks which the nervous system receives from the sur-

Physical determinism stated in the language of the molecular theory of matter.

rounding matter, so that the sensations, feelings and ideas which succeed one another in us can be defined as mechanical resultants, obtained by the compounding of shocks received from without with the previous movements of the atoms of the nervous substance.   But the opposite phenomenon may occur ; and the molecular movements which go on in the nervous system, if compounded with one another or with others, will often give as result-ant a reaction of our organism on its environment : hence the reflex movements, hence also the so-called free and voluntary actions.   As, moreover, the principle of the conservation of energy has been assumed to admit of no exception, there is not an atom, either in the nervous system or in the whole of the universe, whose position is not determined by the sum of the mechanical actions which the other atoms exert upon it.   And the mathematician who knew the position of the molecules or atoms of a human organism at a given moment, as well as the position and motion of all the atoms in the universe capable of influencing it, could calculate with unfailing certainty the past, present and future actions of the person to whom this organism belongs, just as one predicts an astronomical phenom-enon.[1]

We shall not raise any difficulty about recog-

[1] On this point see Lange, *History of Materialism*, Vol. ii, Part ii.

nizing that this conception of physiological phenomena in general, and nervous phenomena in particular, is a very natural
deduction from the law of the conservation of energy. Certainly, the atomic
theory of matter is still at the hypothetical stage, and the purely kinetic explanations of physical facts lose more than they
gain by being too closely bound up with it. We
must observe, however, that, even if we leave aside
the atomic theory as well as any other hypothesis
as to the nature of the ultimate elements of matter,
the necessitating of physiological facts by their
antecedents follows from the theorem of the conservation of energy, as soon as we extend this
theorem to all processes going on in all living bodies.
For to admit the universality of this theorem is to
assume, at bottom, that the material points of
which the universe is composed are subject solely
to forces of attraction and repulsion, arising from
these points themselves and possessing intensities
which depend only on their distances : hence the
relative position of these material points at a given
moment—whatever be their nature—would be
strictly determined by relation to what it was at
the preceding moment. Let us then assume for
a moment that this last hypothesis is true : we
propose to show, in the first place, that it does not
involve the absolute determination of our conscious
states by one another, and then that the very
universality of the principle of the conservation

If principle of conservation of energy is universal, physiological and nervous phenomena are necessitated, but perhaps not conscious states.

L

of energy cannot be admitted except in virtue of some psychological hypothesis.

Even if we assumed that the position, the direction and the velocity of each atom of cerebral *To prove con-* matter are determined at every moment *scious states determined, we* of time, it would not at all follow that our *should have to show a neces-* psychic life is subject to the same neces- *sary connex- ion between* sity. For we should first have to prove *them and cere- bral states.* that a strictly determined psychic state *No such proof.* corresponds to a definite cerebral state, and the proof of this is still to be given. As a rule we do not think of demanding it, because we know that a definite vibration of the tympanum, a definite stimulation of the auditory nerve, gives a definite note on the scale, and because the parallelism of the physical and psychical series has been proved in a fairly large number of cases. But then, nobody has ever contended that we were free, under given conditions, to hear any note or perceive any colour we liked. Sensations of this kind, like many other psychic states, are obviously bound up with certain determining conditions, and it is just for this reason that it has been possible to imagine or discover beneath them a system of movements which obey our abstract mechanics. In short, wherever we succeed in giving a mechanical explanation, we observe a fairly strict parallelism between the physiological and the psychological series, and we need not be surprised at it, since explanations of this kind will assuredly not be met with except where the two series exhibit parallel terms. But to extend this parallelism to the series themselves in their totality is to settle *a priori* the problem of freedom. Certainly this may be done, and some of the greatest thinkers have set the example ; but then, as we said at first, it was not for reasons of a physical order that they asserted the strict correspondence between states of consciousness and modes of extension. Leibniz ascribed it to a pre-established harmony, and would never have admitted that a motion could give rise to a perception as a cause produces an effect. Spinoza said that the modes of thought and the modes of extension correspond with but never influence one another : they only express in two different languages the same eternal truth. But the theories of physical determinism which are rife at the present day are far from displaying the same clearness, the same geometrical rigour. They point to molecular movements taking place in the brain : consciousness is supposed to arise out of these at times in some mysterious way, or rather to follow their track like the phosphorescent line which results from the rubbing of a match. Or yet again we are to think of an invisible musician playing behind the scenes while the actor strikes a keyboard the notes of which yield no sound : consciousness must be supposed to come from an unknown region and to be superimposed on the molecular vibrations, just as the melody is on the rhythmical movements of the actor. But, what-

ever image we fall back upon, we do not prove
and we never shall prove by any reasoning that
the psychic fact is fatally determined by the molecular movement.   For in a movement we may
find the reason of another movement, but not the
reason of a conscious state : only observation
can prove that the latter accompanies the former.
Now the unvarying conjunction of the two
terms has not been verified by experience except
in a very limited number of cases and with regard
to facts which all confess to be almost independent
of the will.   But it is easy to understand why
physical determinism extends this conjunction to
all possible cases.

Consciousness indeed informs us that the majority of our actions can be explained by motives.

Physical
determinism,
when assumed
to be universal,
postulates
psychological
determinism.

But it does not appear that determination here means necessity, since common
sense believes in free will. The determinist, however, led astray by a conception of duration and causality which we shall
criticise a little later, holds that the determination of conscious states by one another is absolute.
This is the origin of associationist determinism,
an hypothesis in support of which the testimony
of consciousness is appealed to, but which cannot,
in the beginning, lay claim to scientific rigour.   It
seems natural that this, so to speak, approximate
determinism, this determinism of quality, should
seek support from the same mechanism that
underlies the phenomena of nature : the latter

would thus convey to the former its own geometrical character, and the transaction would be to the advantage both of psychological determinism, which would emerge from it in a stricter form, and of physical mechanism, which would then spread over everything. A fortunate circumstance favours this alliance. The simplest psychic states do in fact occur as accessories to well-defined physical phenomena, and the greater number of sensations seem to be bound up with definite molecular movements. This mere beginning of an experimental proof is quite enough for the man who, for psychological reasons, is already convinced that our conscious states are the necessary outcome of the circumstances under which they happen. Henceforth he no longer hesitates to hold that the drama enacted in the theatre of consciousness is a literal and even slavish translation of some scenes performed by the molecules and atoms of organized matter. The physical determinism which is reached in this way is nothing but psychological determinism, seeking to verify itself and fix its own outlines by an appeal to the sciences of nature.

But we must own that the amount of freedom which is left to us after strictly complying with the *Is the principle of conservation of energy is rather limited. For, even if this law energy universally valid?* does not exert a necessitating influence over the course of our ideas, it will at least determine our movements. Our inner life will still depend upon ourselves up to a certain point ; but, to an outside observer, there will be nothing to distinguish our activity from absolute automatism.   We are thus led to inquire whether the very extension of the principle of the conservation of energy to all the bodies in nature does not itself involve some psychological theory, and whether the scientist who did not possess *a priori* any prejudice against human freedom would think of setting up this principle as a universal law.

We must not overrate the part played by the principle of the conservation of energy in the his-

It implies that a system can return to its original state. Neglects duration, hence inapplicable to living beings and conscious states.

tory of the natural sciences.   In its present form it marks a certain phase in the evolution of certain sciences ; but it has not been the governing factor in this evolution and we should be wrong in making it the indispensable postulate of all scientific research.   Certainly, every mathematical operation which we carry out on a given quantity implies the permanence of this quantity throughout the course of the operation, in whatever way we may split it up.   In other words, what is given is given, what is not given is not given, and in whatever order we add up the same terms we shall get the same result.   Science will for ever remain subject to this law, which is nothing but the law of non-contradiction ; but this law does not involve any special hypothesis as to the nature of what we ought to take as given, or what will remain constant. No doubt it informs us that something cannot come from nothing ; but experience alone will tell us which aspects or functions of reality must count for something, and which for nothing, from the point of view of positive science. In short, in order to foresee the state of a determinate system at a determinate moment, it is absolutely necessary that something should persist as a constant quantity throughout a series of combinations ; but it belongs to experience to decide as to the nature of this something, and especially to let us know whether it is found in all possible systems, whether, in other words, all possible systems lend themselves to our calculations. It is not certain that all the physicists before Leibniz believed, like Descartes, in the conservation of a fixed quantity of motion in the universe : were their discoveries less valuable on this account or their researches less successful ? Even when Leibniz had substituted for this principle that of the conservation of *vis viva*, it was not possible to regard the law as quite general, since it admitted of an obvious exception in the case of the direct impact of two inelastic bodies. Thus science has done for a very long time without a universal conservative principle. In its present form, and since the development of the mechanical theory of heat, the principle of the conservation of energy certainly seems to apply to the whole range of physico-chemical phenomena. But no one can tell whether the study of physiological phenomena in general, and of nervous phenomena in particular, will not reveal to us, besides the *vis viva* or kinetic energy of which Leibniz spoke, and the potential energy which was a later and necessary adjunct, some new kind of energy which may differ from the other two by rebelling against calculation.   Physical science would not thereby lose any of its exactitude or geometrical rigour, as has lately been asserted : only it would be realized that conservative systems are not the only systems possible, and even, perhaps, that in the whole of concrete reality each of these systems plays the same part as the chemist's atom in bodies and their combinations.   Let us note that the most radical of mechanical theories is that which makes consciousness an *epiphenomenon* which, in given circumstances, may supervene on certain molecular movements.   But, if molecular movement can create sensation out of a zero of consciousness, why should not consciousness in its turn create movement either out of a zero of kinetic and potential energy, or by making use of this energy in its own way ?   Let us also note that the law of the conservation of energy can only be intelligibly applied to a system of which the points, after moving, can return to their former positions. This return is at least conceived of as possible, and it is supposed that under these conditions nothing would be changed in the original state of the system as a whole or of its elements.   In short, time cannot bite into it ; and the instinctive,

though vague, belief of mankind in the conservation of a fixed quantity of matter, a fixed quantity
of energy, perhaps has its root in the very fact that
inert matter does not seem to endure or to preserve
any trace of past time.   But this is not the case
in the realm of life.   Here duration certainly seems
to act like a cause, and the idea of putting things
back in their place at the end of a certain time
involves a kind of absurdity, since such a turning
backwards has never been accomplished in the
case of a living being.   But let us admit that the
absurdity is a mere appearance, and that the
impossibility for living beings to come back to the
past is simply owing to the fact that the physico-
chemical phenomena which take place in living
bodies, being infinitely complex, have no chance
of ever occurring again all at the same time : at
least it will be granted to us that the hypothesis of
a turning backwards is almost meaningless in the
sphere of conscious states.   A sensation, by the
mere fact of being prolonged, is altered to the
point of becoming unbearable.   The same does
not here remain the same, but is reinforced and
swollen by the whole of its past.   In short, while
the material point, as mechanics understands it,
remains in an eternal present, the past is a reality
perhaps for living bodies, and certainly for conscious beings.   While past time is neither a gain
nor a loss for a system assumed to be conservative,
it may be a gain for the living being, and it is
indisputably one for the conscious being.   Such

being the case, is there not much to be said for the hypothesis of a conscious force or free will, which, subject to the action of time and storing up duration, may thereby escape the law of the conservation of energy ?

In truth, it is not a wish to meet the requirements of positive science, but rather a psychological mistake which has caused this abstract principle of mechanics to be set up as a universal law. As we are not accustomed to observe ourselves directly, but perceive ourselves through forms borrowed from the external world, we are led to believe that real duration, the duration lived by consciousness, is the same as the duration which glides over the inert atoms without penetrating and altering them. Hence it is that we do not see any absurdity in putting things back in their place after a lapse of time, in supposing the same motives acting afresh on the same persons, and in concluding that these causes would again produce the same effect. That such an hypothesis has no real meaning is what we shall prove later on. For the present let us simply show that, if once we enter upon this path, we are of course led to set up the principle of the conservation of energy as a universal law. For we have thereby got rid of just that difference between the outer and the inner world which a close examination shows to be the main one : we have identified true duration with apparent duration. After this it would be absurd

The idea of the universality of conservation depends on confusion between concrete duration and abstract time.

to consider time, even *our* time, as a cause of gain
or loss, as a concrete reality, or a force in its own
way. Thus, while we ought only to say (if we
kept aloof from all presuppositions concerning free
will) that the law of the conservation of energy
governs physical phenomena and *may*, one day,
be extended to all phenomena if psychological
facts also prove favourable to it, we go far beyond
this, and, under the influence of a metaphysical
prepossession, we lay down the principle of the
conservation of energy as a law which *should*
govern all phenomena whatever, or must be supposed to do so until psychological facts have
actually spoken against it. Science, properly so
called, has therefore nothing to do with all this.
We are simply confronted with a confusion between
concrete duration and abstract time, two very
different things. In a word, the so-called physical
determinism is reducible at bottom to a psychological determinism, and it is this latter doctrine,
as we hinted at first, that we have to examine.

Psychological determinism, in its latest and
most precise shape, implies an associationist
conception of mind. The existing state
of consciousness is first thought of as
necessitated by the preceding states, but
it is soon realized that this cannot be
a geometrical necessity, such as that which connects a resultant, for example, with its components.
For between successive conscious states there

*Psychological
determinism
depends on as-
sociationist
conception of
mind.*

exists a difference of quality which will always frustrate any attempt to deduce any one of them *a priori* from its predecessors. So experience is appealed to, with the object of showing that the transition from one psychic state to another can always be explained by some simple reason, the second obeying as it were the call of the first. Experience really does show this : and, as for ourselves, we shall willingly admit that there always is some relation between the existing state of consciousness and any new state to which consciousness passes. But is this relation, which explains the transition, the cause of it ?

May we here give an account of what we have personally observed ?   In resuming a conversation

The series of associations may be merely an *ex post facto* attempt to account for a new idea.

which had been interrupted for a few moments we have happened to notice that both we ourselves and our friend were thinking of some new object at the same time.—The reason is, it will be said, that each has followed up for his own part the natural development of the idea at which the conversation had stopped : the same series of associations has been formed on both sides.—No doubt this interpretation holds good in a fairly large number of cases ; careful inquiry, however, has led us to an unexpected result.   It is a fact that the two speakers do connect the new subject of conversation with the former one : they will even point out the intervening ideas ; but, curiously enough, they will not always connect the new idea, which they have both reached, with the same point of the preceding conversation, and the two series of intervening associations may be quite different. What are we to conclude from this, if not that this common idea is due to an unknown cause—perhaps to some physical influence—and that, in order to justify its emergence, it has called forth a series of antecedents which explain it and which seem to be its cause, but are really its effect ?

When a patient carries out at the appointed time the suggestion received in the hypnotic state, the act which he performs is brought about, according to him, by the preceding series of his conscious states. Yet these states are really effects, and not causes : it was necessary that the act should take place ; it was also necessary that the patient should explain it to himself ; and it is the future act which determined, by a kind of attraction, the whole series of psychic states of which it is to be the natural consequence. The determinists will seize on this argument : it proves as a matter of fact that we are sometimes irresistibly subject to another's will. But does it not also show us how our own will is capable of willing for willing's sake, and of then leaving the act which has been performed to be explained by antecedents of which it has really been the cause ?

If we question ourselves carefully, we shall see

(marginal note: Illustration from hypnotic suggestion.)

that we sometimes weigh motives and deliberate over them, when our mind is already made Illustration from delibera-tion. up. An inner voice, hardly perceivable, whispers : " Why this deliberation ? You know the result and you are quite certain of what you are going to do." But no matter ! it seems that we make a point of safe-guarding the principle of mechanism and of conforming to the laws of the association of ideas. The abrupt intervention of the will is a kind of *coup d'état* which our mind foresees and which it tries to legitimate beforehand by a formal deliberation. True, it could be asked whether the will, even when it wills for willing's sake, does not obey some decisive reason, and whether willing for willing's sake is free willing. We shall not insist on this point for the moment. It will be enough for us to have shown that, even when adopting the point of view of associationism, it is difficult to maintain that an act is absolutely determined by its motive and our conscious states by one another. Beneath these deceptive appearances a more attentive psychology sometimes reveals to us effects which precede their causes, and phenomena of psychic attraction which elude the known laws of the association of ideas. But the time has come to ask whether the very point of view which associationism adopts does not involve a defective conception of the self and of the multiplicity of conscious states.

Associationist determinism represents the self as

a collection of psychic states, the strongest of Association- which exerts a prevailing influence and ism involves a defective con- carries the others with it. This doctrine ception of the self. thus sharply distinguishes co-existing psychic phenomena from one another. " I could have abstained from murder," says Stuart Mill, " if my aversion to the crime and my dread of its consequences had been weaker than the temptation which impelled me to commit it."[1] And a little further on : " His desire to do right and his aversion to doing wrong are strong enough to overcome . . . any other desire or aversion which may conflict with them." [2] Thus desire, aversion, fear, temptation are here presented as distinct things which there is no inconvenience in naming separately. Even when he connects these states with the self which experiences them, the English philosopher still insists on setting up clear-cut distinctions : " The conflict is between me and myself ; between (for instance) me desiring a pleasure and me dreading self-reproach." [3] Bain, for his part, devotes a whole chapter to the " Conflict of Motives." [4] In it he balances pleasures and pains as so many terms to which one might attribute, at least by abstraction, an existence of their own. Note that the opponents of determinism agree to follow it into this field. They too speak of associations of ideas and conflicts of

---

[1] Cf. *Examination of Sir W. Hamilton's Philosophy.* 5th ed., (1878), p. 583.   [2] *Ibid.* p. 585.   [3] *Ibid.* p 585.
[4] *The Emotions and the Will*, Chap. vi.

motives, and one of the ablest of these philosophers, Alfred Fouillée, goes so far as to make the idea of freedom itself a motive capable of counterbalancing others.[1] Here, however, lies the danger. Both parties commit themselves to a confusion which arises from language, and which is due to the fact that language is not meant to convey all the delicate shades of inner states.

I rise, for example, to open the window, and I have hardly stood up before I forget what I had to do.—All right, it will be said; you *This erroneous tendency* have associated two ideas, that of an *aided by language. Illustration.* end to be attained and that of a movement to be accomplished: one of the ideas has vanished and only the idea of the movement remains.—However, I do not sit down again; I have a confused feeling that something remains to be done. This particular standing still, therefore, is not the same as any other standing still; in the position which I take up the act to be performed is as it were prefigured, so that I have only to keep this position, to study it, or rather to feel it intimately, in order to recover the idea which had vanished for a moment. Hence, this idea must have tinged with a certain particular colouring the mental image of the intended movement and the position taken up, and this colouring, without doubt, would not have been the same if the end to be attained had been different. Nevertheless

---

[1] Fouillée, *La Liberté et le Déterminisme.*

language would have still expressed the movement and the position in the same way ; and
associationism would have distinguished the two
cases by saying that with the idea of the same
movement there was associated this time the idea
of a new end : as if the mere newness of the end
to be attained did not alter in some degree the
idea of the movement to be performed, even though
the movement itself remained the same ! We
should thus say, not that the image of a certain
position can be connected in consciousness with
images of different ends to be attained, but rather
that positions geometrically identical outside look
different to consciousness from the inside, according to the end contemplated. The mistake of
associationism is that it first did away with the
qualitative element in the act to be peformed and
retained only the geometrical and impersonal
element : with the idea of this act, thus rendered
colourless, it was then necessary to associate some
specific difference to distinguish it from many
other acts. But this association is the work of
the associationist philosopher who is studying my
mind, rather than of my mind itself.

I smell a rose and immediately confused recollections of childhood come back to my memory.
Illustration   In truth, these recollections have not
from "associ-   been called up by the perfume of the
ations" of
smell.   rose : I breathe them in with the very
scent ; it means all that to me. To others it will
smell differently.—It is always the same scent,

M

you will say, but associated with different ideas.—
I am quite willing that you should express yourself in this way ; but do not forget that you have
first removed the personal element from the different impressions which the rose makes on each one
of us ; you have retained only the objective aspect,
that part of the scent of the rose which is public
property and thereby belongs to space.   Only thus
was it possible to give a name to the rose and its
perfume.   You then found it necessary, in order
to distinguish our personal impressions from one
another, to add specific characteristics to the
general idea of rose-scent.   And you now say
that our different impressions, our personal impressions, result from the fact that we associate different recollections with rose-scent.   But the association of which you speak hardly exists except
for you, and as a method of explanation.   It is
in this way that, by setting side by side certain
letters of an alphabet common to a number of
known languages, we may imitate fairly well such
and such a characteristic sound belonging to a
new one ; but not with any of these letters, nor
with all of them, has the sound itself been built up.

We are thus brought back to the distinction
which we set up above between the multiplicity
of juxtaposition and that of fusion or
interpenetration.   Such and such a feeling, such and such an idea, contains an
indefinite plurality of conscious states :
but the plurality will not be observed

Association-
ism fails to
distinguish
between the
multiplicity
of juxtaposi-
tion and that
of fusion.

unless it is, as it were, spread out in this homogeneous medium which some call duration, but which is in reality space. We shall then perceive terms external to one another, and these terms will no longer be the states of consciousness themselves, but their symbols, or, speaking more exactly, the words which express them. There is, as we have pointed out, a close connexion between the faculty of conceiving a homogeneous medium, such as space, and that of thinking by means of general ideas. As soon as we try to give an account of a conscious state, to analyse it, this state, which is above all personal, will be resolved into impersonal elements external to one another, each of which calls up the idea of a genus and is expressed by a word. But because our reason, equipped with the idea of space and the power of creating symbols, draws these multiple elements out of the whole, it does not follow that they were contained in it. For within the whole they did not occupy space and did not care to express themselves by means of symbols ; they permeated and melted into one another. Associationism thus makes the mistake of constantly replacing the concrete phenomenon which takes place in the mind by the artificial reconstruction of it given by philosophy, and of thus confusing the explanation of the fact with the fact itself. We shall perceive this more clearly as we consider deeper and more comprehensive psychic states.

The self comes into contact with the external

world at its surface ; and as this surface retains
the imprint of objects, the self will
Failure of as-
sociationism
to explain the
deeper states
of the self. associate by contiguity terms which it
has perceived in juxtaposition : it is
connexions of this kind, connexions
of quite simple and so to speak impersonal sensations, that the associationist theory fits. But,
just in proportion as we dig below the surface and
get down to the real self, do its states of consciousness cease to stand in juxtaposition and begin to
permeate and melt into one another, and each to be
tinged with the colouring of all the others. Thus
each of us has his own way of loving and hating ;
and this love or this hatred reflects his whole
personality. Language, however, denotes these
states by the same words in every case : so that
it has been able to fix only the objective and
impersonal aspect of love, hate, and the thousand
emotions which stir the soul. We estimate the
talent of a novelist by the power with which he
lifts out of the common domain, to which language
had thus brought them down, feelings and ideas
to which he strives to restore, by adding detail to
detail, their original and living individuality.
But just as we can go on inserting points between
two positions of a moving body without ever filling
up the space traversed, in the same way, by the
mere fact that we associate states with states and
that these states are set side by side instead of
permeating one another, we fail to translate
completely what our soul experiences : there

is no common measure between mind and language.

Therefore, it is only an inaccurate psychology, misled by language, which will show us the soul determined by sympathy, aversion, or hate as though by so many forces pressing upon it. These feelings, provided that they go deep enough, each make up the whole soul, since the whole content of the soul is reflected in each of them. To say that the soul is determined under the influence of any one of these feelings is thus to recognize that it is self-determined. The associationist reduces the self to an aggregate of conscious states : sensations, feelings, and ideas. But if he sees in these various states no more than is expressed in their name, if he retains only their impersonal aspect, he may set them side by side for ever without getting anything but a phantom self, the shadow of the ego projecting itself into space. If, on the contrary, he takes these psychic states with the particular colouring which they assume in the case of a definite person, and which comes to each of them by reflection from all the others, then there is no need to associate a number of conscious states in order to rebuild the person, for the whole personality is in a single one of them, provided that we know how to choose it. And the outward manifestation of this inner state will be just what is called a free act, since the self alone will have been the author

The self is not an aggregate of conscious states. Freedom is self-expression, admitting of degrees, and may be curtailed by education.

of it, and since it will express the whole of the self. Freedom, thus understood, is not *absolute*, as a radically libertarian philosophy would have it ; it admits of degrees. For it is by no means the case that all conscious states blend with one another as raindrops with the water of a lake. The self, in so far as it has to do with a homogeneous space, develops on a kind of surface, and on this surface independent growths may form and float. Thus a suggestion received in the hypnotic state is not incorporated in the mass of conscious states, but, endowed with a life of its own, it will usurp the whole personality when its time comes. A violent anger roused by some accidental circumstance, an hereditary vice suddenly emerging from the obscure depths of the organism to the surface of consciousness, will act almost like a hypnotic suggestion. Alongside these independent elements there may be found more complex series, the terms of which do permeate one another, but which never succeed in blending perfectly with the whole mass of the self. Such is the system of feelings and ideas which are the result of an education not properly assimilated, an education which appeals to the memory rather than to the judgment. Here will be found, within the fundamental self, a parasitic self which continually encroaches upon the other. Many live this kind of life, and die without having known true freedom. But suggestion would become persuasion if the entire self assimilated it ; pas-

sion, even sudden passion, would no longer bear
the stamp of fatality if the whole history of the
person were reflected in it, as in the indignation
of Alceste ; [1] and the most authoritative education
would not curtail any of our freedom if it only
imparted to us ideas and feelings capable of impreg-
nating the whole soul.   It is the whole soul, in
fact, which gives rise to the free decision : and the
act will be so much the freer the more the dynamic
series with which it is connected tends to be the
fundamental self.

Thus understood, free acts are exceptional,
even on the part of those who are most given to
Our every-day controlling and reasoning out what they
acts obey the do.   It has been pointed out that we
laws of asso-
ciation. At generally perceive our own self by
great crises
our decisions refraction through space, that our con-
are really free
as expressing scious states crystallize into words, and
the fundamen-
tal self.   that our living and concrete self thus
gets covered with an outer crust of clean-cut
psychic states, which are separated from one
another and consequently fixed.   We added that,
for the convenience of language and the promotion
of social relations, we have everything to gain by
not breaking through this crust and by assuming
it to give an exact outline of the form of the object
which it covers.   It should now be added that
our daily actions are called forth not so much
by our feelings themselves, which are constantly

---

[1] In Molière's comedy *Le Misanthrope*, (*Tr.*).

changing, as by the unchanging images with which these feelings are bound up. In the morning, when the hour strikes at which I am accustomed to rise, I might receive this impression σὺν ὅλῃ τῇ ψυχῇ, as Plato says ; I might let it blend with the confused mass of impressions which fill my mind ; perhaps in that case it would not determine me to act. But generally this impression, instead of disturbing my whole consciousness like a stone which falls into the water of a pond, merely stirs up an idea which is, so to speak, solidified on the surface, the idea of rising and attending to my usual occupations. This impression and this idea have in the end become tied up with one another, so that the act follows the impression without the self interfering with it. In this instance I am a conscious automaton, and I am so because I have everything to gain by being so. It will be found that the majority of our daily actions are performed in this way and that, owing to the solidification in memory of such and such sensations, feelings, or ideas, impressions from the outside call forth movements on our part which, though conscious and even intelligent, have many points of resemblance with reflex acts. It is to these acts, which are very numerous but for the most part insignificant, that the associationist theory is applicable. They are, taken all together, the substratum of our free activity, and with respect to this activity they play the same part as our organic functions in relation to the whole of our conscious life. Moreover we will grant to determinism that we often resign our freedom in more serious circumstances, and that, by sluggishness or indolence, we allow this same local process to run its course when our whole personality ought, so to speak, to vibrate. When our most trustworthy friends agree in advising us to take some important step, the sentiments which they utter with so much insistence lodge on the surface of our ego and there get solidified in the same way as the ideas of which we spoke just now. Little by little they will form a thick crust which will cover up our own sentiments ; we shall believe that we are acting freely, and it is only by looking back to the past, later on, that we shall see how much we were mistaken. But then, at the very minute when the act is going to be performed, *something* may revolt against it. It is the deep-seated self rushing up to the surface. It is the outer crust bursting, suddenly giving way to an irresistible thrust. Hence in the depths of the self, below this most reasonable pondering over most reasonable pieces of advice, something else was going on—a gradual heating and a sudden boiling over of feelings and ideas, not unperceived, but rather unnoticed. If we turn back to them and carefully scrutinize our memory, we shall see that we had ourselves shaped these ideas, ourselves lived these feelings, but that, through some strange reluctance to exercise our will, we had thrust them back into the darkest depths of our soul

whenever they came up to the surface. And this
is why we seek in vain to explain our sudden
change of mind by the visible circumstances which
preceded it. We wish to know the reason why
we have made up our mind, and we find that we
have decided without any reason, and perhaps
even against every reason. But, in certain cases,
that is the best of reasons. For the action which
has been performed does not then express some
superficial idea, almost external to ourselves,
distinct and easy to account for : it agrees with
the whole of our most intimate feelings, thoughts
and aspirations, with that particular conception
of life which is the equivalent of all our past
experience, in a word, with our personal idea of
happiness and of honour. Hence it has been a
mistake to look for examples in the ordinary and
even indifferent circumstances of life in order
to prove that man is capable of choosing without
a motive. It might easily be shown that these
insignificant actions are bound up with some
determining reason. It is at the great and solemn
crisis, decisive of our reputation with others, and
yet more with ourselves, that we choose in defiance
of what is conventionally called a motive, and
this absence of any tangible reason is the more
striking the deeper our freedom goes.

But the determinist, even when he refrains
from regarding the more serious emotions or deep-
seated psychic states as forces, nevertheless distinguishes them from one another and is thus

led to a mechanical conception of the self. He

Determinism
sets on the
one side the
ego, always
self-identical,
and on the
other con-
trary feelings.
But this is mere
symbolism.
will show us this self hesitating between two contrary feelings, passing from one to the other and finally deciding in favour of one of them. The self and the feelings which stir it are thus treated as well defined objects, which remain

identical during the whole of the process. But if it is always the same self which deliberates, and if the two opposite feelings by which it is moved do not change, how, in virtue of this very principle of causality which determinism appeals to, will the self ever come to a decision ? The truth is that the self, by the mere fact of experiencing the first feeling, has already changed to a slight extent when the second supervenes : all the time that the deliberation is going on, the self is changing and is consequently modifying the two feelings which agitate it. A dynamic series of states is thus formed which permeate and strengthen one another, and which will lead by a natural evolution to a free act. But determinism, ever craving for symbolical representation, cannot help substituting words for the opposite feelings which share the ego between them, as well as for the ego itself. By giving first the person and then the feelings by which he is moved a fixed form by means of sharply defined words, it deprives them in advance of every kind of living activity. It will then see on the one side an ego always self-identical, and on the other contrary feelings, also self-identical, which dispute for its possession ; victory will necessarily belong to the stronger. But this mechanism, to which we have condemned ourselves in advance, has no value beyond that of a symbolical representation : it cannot hold good against the witness of an attentive consciousness, which shows us inner dynamism as a fact.

In short, we are free when our acts spring from our whole personality, when they express it, when **Freedom and** they have that indefinable resemblance **character. The** to it which one sometimes finds between **determinist** **next asks,** the artist and his work. It is no use **could our act** **have been dif-** asserting that we are then yielding to **ferent or can** **it be foretold ?** the all-powerful influence of our character. Our character is still ourselves ; and because we are pleased to split the person into two parts so that by an effort of abstraction we may consider in turn the self which feels or thinks and the self which acts, it would be very strange to conclude that one of the two selves is coercing the other. Those who ask whether we are free to alter our character lay themselves open to the same objection. Certainly our character is altering imperceptibly every day, and our freedom would suffer if these new acquisitions were grafted on to our self and not blended with it. But, as soon as this blending takes place, it must be admitted that the change which has supervened in our character belongs to us, that we have appropriated it. In a word, if it is agreed to call every act free which springs from the self and from the self alone, the act which bears the mark of our personality is truly free, for our self alone will lay claim to its paternity. It would thus be recognized that free will is a fact, if it were agreed to look for it in a certain characteristic of the decision which is taken, in the free act itself. But the determinist feeling that he cannot retain his hold on this position, takes refuge in the past or the future. Sometimes he transfers himself in thought to some earlier period and asserts the necessary determination, from this very moment, of the act which is to come ; sometimes, assuming in advance that the act is already performed, he claims that it could not have taken place in any other way. The opponents of determinism themselves willingly follow it on to this new ground and agree to introduce into their definition of our free act —perhaps not without some risk—the anticipation of what we might do and the recollection of some other decision which we might have taken. It is advisable, then, that we should place ourselves at this new point of view, and, setting aside all translation into words, all symbolism in space, attend to what pure consciousness alone shows us about an action that has come to pass or an action which is still to come. The original error of determinism and the mistake of its opponents will thus be grasped on another side, in so far as they bear explicitly on a certain misconception of duration.

" To be conscious of free will," says Stuart

Mill, " must mean to be conscious, before I have
decided, that I am able to decide either
way." [1] This is really the way in which
the defenders of free will understand it ;
and they assert that when we perform an action
freely, some other action would have been "equally
possible." On this point they appeal to the testimony of consciousness, which shows us, beyond
the act itself, the power of deciding in favour of
the opposite course. Inversely, determinism claims
that, given certain antecedents, only one resultant
action was possible. " When we think of ourselves hypothetically," Stuart Mill goes on, " as
having acted otherwise than we did, we always
suppose a difference in the antecedents. We picture ourselves as having known something that
we did not know, or not known something that
we did know." [2] And, faithful to his principle,
the English philosopher assigns consciousness the
rôle of informing us about what is, not about what
might be. We shall not insist for the moment on
this last point : we reserve the question in what
sense the ego perceives itself as a determining
cause. But beside this psychological question
there is another, belonging rather to metaphysics,
which the determinists and their opponents solve
a priori along opposite lines. The argument of

---

[1] *Examination of Sir W. Hamilton's Philosophy.* 5th ed.,
(1878), p. 580.

[2] *Ibid.* p. 583.

the former implies that there is only one possible act corresponding to given antecedents : the believers in free will assume, on the other hand, that the same series could issue in several different acts, equally possible. It is on this question of the equal possibility of two contrary actions or volitions that we shall first dwell : perhaps we shall thus gather some indication as to the nature of the operation by which the will makes its choice.

I hesitate between two possible actions X and Y, and I go in turn from one to the other. This means that I pass through a series of *Geometrical (and thereby deceptive) representation of the process of coming to a decision.* states, and that these states can be divided into two groups according as I incline more towards X or in the contrary direction. Indeed, these opposite inclinations alone have a real existence, and X and Y are two symbols by which I represent at their arrival- or termination-points, so to speak, two different tendencies of my personality at successive moments of duration. Let us then rather denote the tendencies themselves by X and Y ; will this new notation give a more faithful image of the concrete reality ? It must be noticed, as we said above, that the self grows, expands, and changes as it passes through the two contrary states : if not, how would it ever come to a decision ? Hence there are not exactly two contrary states, but a large number of successive and different states within which I distinguish, by an effort of imagination, two opposite directions. Thus we shall get still nearer the reality by agreeing to use the invariable signs X and Y to denote, not these tendencies or states themselves, since they are constantly changing, but the two different directions which our imagination ascribes to them for the greater convenience of language. It will also be understood that these are symbolical representations, that in reality there are not two tendencies, or even two directions, but a self which lives and develops by means of its very hesitations, until the free action drops from it like an over-ripe fruit.

But this conception of voluntary activity does not satisfy common sense, because, being essentially a devotee of mechanism, it loves clear-cut distinctions, those which are expressed by sharply defined words or by different positions in space. Hence it will picture a self which, after having traversed a series M O of conscious states, when it reaches the point O finds before it two directions O X and O Y, equally open. These directions thus become *things*, real paths into which the highroad of consciousness leads, and it depends only on the self which of them is entered upon. In short, the continuous and living activity of this self, in which we have dis-

The only reality is the living developing self, in which we distinguish by abstraction two opposite tendencies or directions.

tinguished, by abstraction only, two opposite directions, is replaced by these directions themselves, transformed into indifferent inert things awaiting our choice.   But then we must certainly transfer the activity of the self somewhere or other.   We will put it, according to this hypothesis, at the point O : we will say that the self, when it reaches O and finds two courses open to it, hesitates, deliberates and finally decides in favour of one of them.   As we find it difficult to picture the double direction of the conscious activity in all the phases of its continuous development, we separate off these two tendencies on the one hand and the activity of the self on the other : we thus get an impartially active ego hesitating between two inert and, as it were, solidified courses of action.   Now, if it decides in favour of O X, the line O Y will nevertheless remain ; if it chooses O Y, the path O X will remain open, waiting in case the self retraces its steps in order to make use of it.   It is in this sense that we say, when speaking of a free act, that the contrary action was equally possible.   And, even if we do not draw a geometrical figure on paper, we involuntarily and almost unconsciously think of it as soon as we distinguish in the free act a number of successive phases, the *conception* of opposite motives, *hesitation* and *choice*—thus hiding the geometrical symbolism under a kind of verbal crystallization.   Now it is easy to see that this really mechanical conception of freedom

N

issues naturally and logically in the most unbending determinism.

The living activity of the self, in which we distinguish by abstraction two opposite tend-encies, will finally issue either at X or Y. Now, since it is agreed to localize the double activity of the self at the point O, there is no reason to separate this activity from the act in which it will issue and which forms part and parcel of it. And if experience shows that the decision has been in favour of X, it is not a neutral activity which should be placed at the point O, but an activity tending in advance in the direction O X, in spite of apparent hesitations. If, on the contrary, observation proves that the decision has been in favour of Y, we must infer that the activity localized by us at the point O was bent in this second direction in spite of some oscillations towards the first. To assert that the self, when it reaches the point O, chooses indifferently between X and Y, is to stop half way in the course of our geometrical symbolism ; it is to separate off at the point O only a part of this continuous activity in which we undoubtedly distinguished two different directions, but which in addition has gone on to X or Y : why not take this last fact into account as well as the other two ? Why not assign it the place that belongs to it in the symbolical figure which we have just constructed ? But if the self, when it reaches the point O, is already

If this symbolism represents the facts, the activity of the self has always tended in *one* direction, and determinism results.

determined in one direction, there is no use in the other way remaining open, the self cannot take it. And the same rough symbolism which was meant to show the contingency of the action performed, ends, by a natural extension, in proving its absolute necessity.

In short, defenders and opponents of free will agree in holding that the action is preceded by a kind of mechanical oscillation between *Libertarians ignore the fact that one path has been chosen, and not the other.* the two points X and Y. If I decide in favour of X, the former will tell me : you hesitated and deliberated, therefore Y was possible. The others will answer : you chose X, therefore you had some reason for doing so, and those who declare that Y was equally possible forget this reason : they leave aside one of the conditions of the problem. Now, if I dig deeper underneath these two opposite solutions, I discover a common postulate : both take up their position after the action X has been performed, and represent the process of my voluntary activity by a path M O which branches off at the point O, the lines O X and O Y symbolizing the two directions which abstraction distinguishes within the continuous activity of which X is the goal. But while the determinists take account of all that they know, and note that the path M O X has been traversed, their opponents mean to ignore one of the data with which they have constructed the figure, and after having traced out the lines O X and O Y, which should together represent the progress of the activity of the self, they bring back the self to the point O to oscillate there until further orders.

It should not be forgotten, indeed, that the figure, which is really a splitting of our psychic activity in space, is purely symbolical, and, as such, cannot be constructed unless we adopt the hypothesis that our deliberation is finished and our mind made up. If you trace it beforehand, you assume that you have reached the end and are present in imagination at the final act. In short this figure does not show me the deed in the doing but the deed already done. Do not ask me then whether the self, having traversed the path M O and decided in favour of X, could or could not choose Y : I should answer that the question is meaningless, because there is no line M O, no point O, no path O X, no direction O Y. To ask such a question is to admit the possibility of adequately representing time by space and a succession by a simultaneity. It is to ascribe to the figure we have traced the value of a description, and not merely of a symbol; it is to believe that it is possible to follow the process of psychic activity on this figure like the march of an army on a map. We have been present at the deliberation of the self in all its phases until the act was performed: then, recapitulating the terms of the series, we perceive succession under the form of simultaneity, we project

But the figure merely gives the stereotyped memory of the process, and not the dynamic progress which issued in the act.

time into space, and we base our reasoning, con-
sciously or unconsciously, on this geometrical
figure. But this figure represents a *thing* and not
a *progress* ; it corresponds, in its inertness, to a
kind of stereotyped memory of the whole process
of deliberation and the final decision arrived at :
how could it give us the least idea of the concrete
movement, the dynamic progress by which the
deliberation issued in the act ? And yet, once
the figure is constructed, we go back in imagination into the past and will have it that our psychic
activity has followed exactly the path traced out
by the figure. We thus fall into the mistake which
has been pointed out above : we give a mechanical
explanation of a fact, and then substitute the
explanation for the fact itself. Hence we encounter insuperable difficulties from the very beginning : if the two courses were equally possible, how
have we made our choice ? If only one of them
was possible, why did we believe ourselves free ?
And we do not see that both questions come back
to this : Is time space ?

If I glance over a road marked on the map
and follow it up to a certain point, there is
Fundamental nothing to prevent my turning back and
error is con-
fusion of time trying to find out whether it branches
and space.
The self infal- off anywhere. But time is not a line
lible in affirm-
ing immedi- along which one can pass again. Cer-
ate experience
of freedom, tainly, once it has elapsed, we are justi-
but cannot ex-
plain it. fied in picturing the successive moments
as external to one another and in thus thinking

of a line traversing space ; but it must then be understood that this line does not symbolize the time which is passing but the time which has passed. Defenders and opponents of free will alike forget this—the former when they assert, and the latter when they deny the possibility of acting differently from what we have done. The former reason thus : " The path is not yet traced out, therefore it may take any direction whatever." To which the answer is : " You forget that it is not possible to speak of a path till the action is performed : but then it will have been traced out." The latter say : " The path has been traced out in such and such a way : therefore its possible direction was not any direction whatever, but only this one direction." To which the answer is : " Before the path was traced out there was no direction, either possible or impossible, for the very simple reason that there could not yet be any question of a path." Get rid of this clumsy symbolism, the idea of which besets you without your knowing it ; you will see that the argument of the determinists assumes this puerile form : " The act, once performed, is performed," and that their opponents reply : " The act, before being performed, was not yet performed." In other words, the question of freedom remains after this discussion exactly where it was to begin with ; nor must we be sur- prised at it, since freedom must be sought in a certain shade or quality of the action itself and not in the relation of this act to what it is not or to what it might have been. All the difficulty arises from the fact that both parties picture the deliberation under the form of an oscillation in space, while it really consists in a dynamic progress in which the self and its motives, like real living beings, are in a constant state of becoming. The self, infallible when it affirms its immediate experiences, feels itself free and says so ; but, as soon as it tries to explain its freedom to itself, it no longer perceives itself except by a kind of refraction through space. Hence a symbolism of a mechanical kind, equally incapable of proving, disproving, or illustrating free will.

But determinism will not admit itself beaten, and, putting the question in a new form, it will **Is prediction of an act possible? Probable and infallible conclusions.** say : " Let us leave aside actions already performed : let us consider only actions that are to come. The question is whether, knowing from now onwards all the future antecedents, some higher intelligence would not be able to predict with absolute certainty the decision which will result." —We gladly agree to the question being put in these terms : it will give us a chance of stating our own theory with greater precision. But we shall first draw a distinction between those who think that the knowledge of antecedents would enable us to state a *probable* conclusion and those who speak of an *infallible* foresight. To say that a certain friend, under certain circumstances, will very probably act in a certain way, is not so much to predict the future conduct of our friend as to pass a judgment on his present character, that is to say, on his past. Although our feelings, our ideas, our character, are constantly altering, a sudden change is seldom observed ; and it is still more seldom that we cannot say of a person whom we know that certain actions seem to accord fairly well with his nature and that certain others are absolutely inconsistent with it. All philosophers will agree on this point ; for to say that a given action is consistent or inconsistent with the present character of a person whom one knows is not to bind the future to the present. But the determinist goes much further : he asserts that our solution is provisional simply because we never know all the conditions of the problem ; that our forecast would gain in probability in proportion as we were provided with a larger number of these conditions ; that, therefore, complete and perfect knowledge of all the antecedents without any exception would make our forecast infallibly true. Such, then, is the hypothesis which we have to examine.

For the sake of greater definiteness, let us imagine a person called upon to make a seemingly free decision under serious circumstances; *To know com-* we shall call him Peter. The question *pletely the* *antecedents* we shall call him Peter. The question *and conditions* *of an action is* is whether a philosopher Paul, living at *to be actually* *performing it:* the same period as Peter, or, if you prefer, a few centuries before, would have been able, knowing *all* the conditions under which Peter acts, to foretell with certainty the choice which Peter made.

There are several ways of picturing the mental condition of a person at a given moment. We try to do it when e.g. we read a novel ; but whatever care the author may have taken in depicting the feelings of his hero, and even in tracing back his history, the end, foreseen or unforeseen, will add something to the idea which we had formed of the character : the character, therefore, was only imperfectly known to us. In truth, the deeper psychic states, those which are translated by free acts, express and sum up the whole of our past history : if Paul knows all the conditions under which Peter acts, we must suppose that no detail of Peter's life escapes him, and that his imagination reconstructs and even lives over again Peter's history. But we must here make a vital distinction. When I myself pass through a certain psychic state, I know exactly the intensity of this state and its importance in relation to the others, not by measurement or comparison, but because the intensity of e.g. a deep-seated feeling is nothing else than the feeling itself. On the other hand, if I try to give you an account of this psychic state, I shall be unable to make you realize its intensity except by some definite sign of a mathematical kind : I shall have to measure its importance, compare it with what goes before and what follows, in short determine the part which it plays in the final act. And I shall say that it is more or less intense, more or less important, according as the final act is explained by it or apart from it. On the other hand, for my own consciousness, which perceived this inner state, there was no need of a comparison of this kind : the intensity was given to it as an inexpressible quality of the state itself. In other words, the intensity of a psychic state is not given to consciousness as a special sign accompanying this state and denoting its power, like an exponent in algebra ; we have shown above that it expresses rather its shade, its characteristic colouring, and that, if it is a question of a feeling, for example, its intensity consists in being felt. Hence we have to distinguish two ways of assimilating the conscious states of other people : the one dynamic, which consists in experiencing them oneself ; the other static, which consists in substituting for the consciousness of these states their image or rather their intellectual symbol, their idea. In this case the conscious states are *imagined* instead of being *reproduced* ; but, then, to the image of the psychic states themselves some indication of their *intensity* should be added, since they no longer act on the person in whose mind they are pictured and the latter has no longer any chance of experiencing their force by actually feeling them. Now, this indication itself will necessarily assume a quantitative character : it will be pointed out, for example, that a certain feeling has more strength than another feeling, that it is necessary to take more account of it, that it has played a greater part ; and how could this be known unless the later history of the person were known in advance, with the precise actions in which this multiplicity of states or inclinations has issued ? Therefore, if Paul is to have an adequate idea of Peter's state at any moment of his history, there are only two courses open ; either, like a novelist who knows whither he is conducting his characters, Paul must already know Peter's final act, and must thus be able to supplement his mental image of the successive states through which Peter is going to pass by some indication of their value in relation to the whole of Peter's history ; or he must make up his mind to pass through these different states, not in imagination, but in reality. The former hypothesis must be put on one side since the very point at issue is whether, the antecedents *alone* being given, Paul will be able to foresee the final act. We find ourselves compelled, therefore, to alter radically the idea which we had formed of Paul : he is not, as we had thought at first, a spectator whose eyes pierce the future, but an actor who plays Peter's part in advance. And notice that you cannot exempt him from any detail of this part, for the most common-place events have their importance in a life-story ; and even supposing that they have not, you cannot decide that they are insignificant except in relation to the final act, which, by hypothesis, is not given. Neither have you the right to cut short—were it only by a second—the different states of consciousness through which Paul is going to pass before Peter ; for the effects of the same feeling, for example, go on accumulating at every moment of duration, and the sum total of these effects could not be realized all at once unless one knew the importance of the feeling, taken in its totality, in relation to the final act, which is the very thing that is supposed to remain unknown. But if Peter and Paul have experienced the same feelings in the same order, if their minds have the same history, how will you distinguish one from the other ? Will it be by the body in which they dwell ? They would then always differ in some respect, viz., that at no moment of their history would they have a mental picture of the same body. Will it be by the place which they occupy in time ? In that case they would no longer be present at the same events : now, by hypothesis, they have the same past and the same present, having the same experience. You must now make up your mind about it : Peter and Paul are one and the same person, whom you call Peter when he acts and Paul when you recapitulate his history. The more complete you made the sum of the conditions which, when known, would have enabled you to predict Peter's future action, the closer became your grasp of his existence and the nearer you came to living his life over again down to its smallest details : you thus reached the very moment when, the action taking place, there was no longer anything to be foreseen, but only something to be done.   Here again any attempt to reconstruct ideally an act really *willed* ends in the mere witnessing of the act whilst it is being performed or when it is already done.

Hence it is a question devoid of meaning to ask : Could or could not the act be foreseen, given the sum total of its antecedents?

Hence meaningless to ask whether an act can be foreseen when *all* its antecedents are given.

For there are two ways of assimilating these antecedents, the one dynamic the other static.   In the first case we shall be led by imperceptible steps to identify ourselves with the person we are dealing with, to pass through the same series of states, and thus to get back to the very moment at which the act is performed ; hence there can no longer be any question of foreseeing it.   In the second case, we presuppose the final act by the mere fact of annexing to the qualitative description of the previous states the quantitative appreciation of their importance.   Here again the one party is led merely to realize that the act is not yet performed when it is to be performed, and the other, that when performed it is performed.   This, like the previous discussion, leaves the question of freedom exactly where it was to begin with.

By going deeper into this twofold argument, we

shall find, at its very root, the two fundamental illusions of the reflective consciousness.

The two falla-
cies involved:
(1) regarding
intensity as a
magnitude,
not a quality;
(2)substituting
material
symbol for
dynamic pro-
cess.
The first consists in regarding intensity as a mathematical property of psychic states and not, as we said at the beginning of this essay, as a special quality, as a particular shade of these various states. The second consists in substituting for the concrete reality or dynamic progress, which consciousness perceives, the material symbol of this progress when it has already reached its end, that is to say, of the act already accomplished together with the series of its antecedents. Certainly, once the final act is completed, I can ascribe to all the antecedents their proper value, and picture the interplay of these various elements as a conflict or a composition of forces. But to ask whether, the antecedents being known as well as their value, one could foretell the final act, is to beg the question ; it is to forget that we cannot know the value of the antecedents without knowing the final act, which is the very thing that is not yet known ; it is to suppose wrongly that the symbolical diagram which we draw in our own way for representing the action *when completed* has been drawn by the action itself *whilst progressing*, and drawn by it in an automatic manner.

Now, in these two illusions themselves a third one is involved, and you will see that the question whether the act could or could not be foreseen always comes back to this : Is time space ?

You begin by setting side by side in some ideal space the conscious states which suc-

Claiming to foresee an action always comes back to confusing time with space.

ceed one another in Peter's mind, and you perceive his life as a kind of path M O X Y traced out by a moving body M in space. You then blot out in thought the part O X Y of this curve, and you inquire whether, knowing M O, you would have been able to determine the portion O X of the curve which the moving body describes beyond O. Such is, in the main, the question which you put when you

bring in a philosopher Paul, who lives before Peter and has to picture to himself the conditions under which Peter will act. You thus materialize these conditions ; you make the time to come into a road already marked out across the plain, which we can contemplate from the top of the mountain, even if we have not traversed it and are never to do so. But, now, you soon notice that the know-ledge of the part M O of the curve would not be enough, unless you were shown the position of the points of this line, not only in relation to one another, but also in relation to the points of the whole line M O X Y ; which would amount to being given in advance the very elements which have to be determined. So you then alter your hypo-thesis ; you realize that time does not require to be seen, but to be lived ; and hence you conclude that, if your knowledge of the line M O was not a sufficient datum, the reason must have been that you looked at it from the outside instead of identifying yourself with the point M, which describes not only M O but also the whole curve, and thus making its movement your own. Therefore, you persuade Paul to come and coincide with Peter ; and naturally, then, it is the line M O X Y which Paul traces out in space, since, by hypothesis, Peter describes this line. But in no wise do you prove thus that Paul foresaw Peter's action ; you only show that Peter acted in the way he did, since Paul became Peter. It is true that you then come back, unwittingly, to your former hypothesis, because you continually confuse the line M O X Y in its tracing with the line M O X Y already traced, that is to say, time with space. After causing Paul to come down and identify himself with Peter as long as was required, you let him go up again and resume his former post of observation. No wonder if he then perceives the line M O X Y complete : he himself has just been completing it.

What makes the confusion a natural and almost an unavoidable one is that science seems to point to many cases where we do anticipate the future. Do we not determine be-

Confusion arising from prediction of astronomical phenomena. forehand the conjunctions of heavenly bodies, solar and lunar eclipses, in short the greater number of astronomical phenomena ? Does not, then, the human intellect embrace in the present moment immense intervals of duration still to come ? No doubt it does ; but an anticipation of this kind has not the slightest resemblance to the anticipation of a voluntary act. Indeed, as we shall see, the reasons which render it possible to foretell an astronomical phenomenon are the very ones which prevent us from determining in advance an act which springs from our free activity. For the future of the material universe, although contemporaneous with the future of a conscious being, has no analogy to it.

In order to put our finger on this vital difference, let us assume for a moment that some mischievous *Illustration from hypothetical acceleration of physical movements.* genius, more powerful still than the mischievous genius conjured up by Descartes, decreed that all the movements of the universe should go twice as fast. There would be no change in astronomical phenomena, or at any rate in the equations which enable us to foresee them, for in these equations the symbol t does not stand for a duration, but for a relation between two durations, for a certain number of units of time, in short, for a certain number of *simultaneities :* these simultaneities, these coincidences would still take place in equal number : only the intervals which separate them would have diminished, but these intervals never make their appearance in our calculations. Now these intervals are just duration *lived*, duration which our consciousness perceives, and our consciousness would soon inform us of a shortening of the day if we had not experienced the usual amount of duration between sunrise and sunset. No doubt it would not measure this shortening, and perhaps it would not even perceive it immediately as a change of quantity ; but it would realize in some way or other a decline in the usual storing up of experience, a change in the progress usually accomplished between sunrise and sunset.

Now, when an astronomer foretells e.g. a lunar eclipse, he merely exercises in his own way the power which we have ascribed to our mischievous genius. He decrees that time shall go ten times, a hundred times, a thousand times as fast, and he has a right to do so, since all that he thus changes is the nature of the conscious intervals, and since these intervals, by hypothesis, do not enter into the calculations. Therefore, into a psychological duration of a few seconds he may put several years, even several centuries of astronomical time : that is his procedure when he traces in advance the path of a heavenly body or represents it by an equation. What he does is nothing but establishing a series of relations of position between this body and other given bodies, a series of simultaneities and coincidences, a series of numerical relations : as for duration properly so called, it remains outside the calculation and could only be perceived by a consciousness capable of living through the intervals and, in fact, living the intervals themselves, instead of merely perceiving their extremities. Indeed it is even conceivable that this

Astronomical prophecy such an acceleration.

consciousness could live so slow and lazy a life as to take in the whole path of the heavenly body in a single perception, just as we do when we perceive the successive positions of a shooting star as one line of fire. Such a consciousness would find itself really in the same conditions in which the astronomer places himself ideally ; it would see in the present what the astronomer perceives in the future. In truth, if the latter foresees a future phenomenon, it is only on condition of making it to a certain extent a present phenomenon, or at least of enormously reducing the interval which separates us from it. In short, the time of which we speak in astronomy is a number, and the nature of the units of this number cannot be specified in our calculations ; we may therefore assume them to be as small as we please, provided that the same hypothesis is extended to the whole series of operations, and that the successive relations of position in space are thus preserved. We shall then be present in imagination at the phenomenon we wish to foretell ; we shall know exactly at what point in space and after how many units of time this phenomenon takes place ; if we then restore to these units their psychical nature, we shall thrust the event again into the future and say that we have foreseen it, when in reality we have seen it.

But these units of time which make up living duration, and which the astronomer can dispose of as he pleases because they give no handle to

science, are just what concern the psychologist,
In dealing for psychology deals with the intervals
with states of
consciousness themselves and not with their extrem-
we cannot
vary their du- ities. Certainly pure consciousness does
ration without
altering their not perceive time as a sum of units of
nature. duration : left to itself, it has no means
and even no reason to measure time ; but a feeling
which lasted only half the number of days, for
example, would no longer be the same feeling
for it ; it would lack thousands of impressions
which gradually thickened its substance and
altered its colour. True, when we give this feeling
a certain name, when we treat it as a thing, we
believe that we can diminish its duration by half,
for example, and also halve the duration of all the
rest of our history : it seems that it would still
be the same life, only on a reduced scale. But we
forget that states of consciousness are processes,
and not things ; that if we denote them each by a
single word, it is for the convenience of language ;
that they are alive and therefore constantly changing ; that, in consequence, it is impossible to cut
off a moment from them without making them
poorer by the loss of some impression, and thus
altering their quality. I quite understand that
the orbit of a planet might be perceived all at
once or in a very short time, because its successive
positions or the *results* of its movement are the
only things that matter, and not the duration of
the equal intervals which separate them. But
when we have to do with a feeling, it has no precise

result except its having been felt ; and, to estimate
this result adequately, it would be necessary to
have gone through all the phases of the feeling
itself and to have taken up the same duration.
Even if this feeling has finally issued in some definite action, which might be compared to the
definite position of a planet in space, the knowledge of this act will hardly enable us to estimate
the influence of the feeling on the whole of a life-
story, and it is this very influence which we want
to know. All foreseeing is in reality seeing, and
this seeing takes place when we can reduce as
much as we please an interval of future time while
preserving the relation of its parts to one another,
as happens in the case of astronomical predictions.
But what does reducing an interval of time mean,
except emptying or impoverishing the conscious
states which fill it ?   And does not the very
possibility of seeing an astronomical period in
miniature thus imply the impossibility of modifying a psychological series in the same way, since
it is only by taking this psychological series as an
invariable basis that we shall be able to make an
astronomical period vary arbitrarily as regards
the unit of duration ?

Thus, when we ask whether a future action
could have been foreseen, we unwittingly identify

**Difference be-
tween past and
future dura-
tion in this
respect.**
that time with which we have to do in
the exact sciences, and which is reducible
to a number, with real duration, whose
so-called quantity is really a quality,

and which we cannot curtail by an instant without altering the nature of the facts which fill it. No doubt the identification is made easier by the fact that in a large number of cases we are justified in dealing with real duration as with astronomical time. Thus, when we call to mind the past, i.e. a series of deeds done, we always shorten it, without however distorting the nature of the event which interests us. The reason is that we know it already ; for the psychic state, when it reaches the end of the *progress* which constitutes its very existence, becomes a *thing* which one can picture to oneself all at once. Here we find ourselves in the same position as the astronomer, when he takes in at a glance the orbit which a planet will need several years to traverse. In fact, astronomical prediction should be compared with the recollection of the past state of consciousness, not with the anticipation of the future one. But when we have to determine a future state of consciousness, however superficial it may be, we can no longer view the antecedents in a static condition as things ; we must view them in a dynamic condition as processes, since we are concerned with their influence alone. Now their duration is this very influence. Therefore it will no longer do to shorten future duration in order to picture its parts beforehand ; one is bound to *live* this duration whilst it is unfolding. As far as deep-seated psychic states are concerned, there is no perceptible difference between foreseeing, seeing, and acting.

Only one course will remain open to the determinist. He will probably give up asserting the possibility of foreseeing a certain future act or state of consciousness, but will maintain that every act is determined by its psychic antecedents, or, in other words, that the facts of consciousness, like the phenomena of nature, are subject to laws. This way of arguing means, at bottom, that he will leave out the particular features of the concrete psychic states, lest he find himself confronted by phenomena which defy all symbolical representation and therefore all anticipation. The particular nature of these phenomena is thus thrust out of sight, but it is asserted that, being phenomena, they must remain subject to the law of causality. Now, it is argued, this law means that every phenomenon is determined by its conditions, or, in other words, that the same causes produce the same effects. Either, then, the act is inseparably bound to its antecedents, or the principle of causality admits of an incomprehensible exception.

The determinist argument that psychic phenomena are subject to the law "same antecedents, same consequent."

This last form of the determinist argument differs less than might be thought from all the others which have been examined above. To say that the same inner causes will reproduce the same effects is to assume that the same cause can appear a second time on the stage of consciousness. Now, if duration is what we say, deep-

But as regards inner states the same antecedents will never recur.

seated psychic states are radically heterogeneous
to each other, and it is impossible that any two of
them should be quite alike, since they are two
different moments of a life-story. While the
external object does not bear the mark of the time
that has elapsed and thus, in spite of the difference of time, the physicist can again encounter
identical elementary conditions, duration is something real for the consciousness which preserves
the trace of it, and we cannot here speak of identical conditions, because the same moment does
not occur twice. It is no use arguing that, even
if there are no two deep-seated psychic states
which are altogether alike, yet analysis would
resolve these different states into more general
and homogeneous elements which might be compared with each other. This would be to forget
that even the simplest psychic elements possess
a personality and a life of their own, however
superficial they may be ; they are in a constant
state of becoming, and the same feeling, by
the mere fact of being repeated, is a new feeling.
Indeed, we have no reason for calling it by its
former name save that it corresponds to the same
external cause or projects itself outwardly into
similar attitudes : hence it would simply be beg-
ging the question to deduce from the so-called
likeness of two conscious states that the same cause
produces the same effect. In short, if the causal
relation still holds good in the realm of inner states,
it cannot resemble in any way what we call

causality in nature. For the physicist, the same cause always produces the same effect : for a psychologist who does not let himself be misled by merely apparent analogies, a deep-seated inner cause produces its effect once for all and will never reproduce it. And if it is now asserted that this effect was inseparably bound up with this particular cause, such an assertion will mean one of two things : either that, the antecedents being given, the future action might have been foreseen ; or that, the action having once been performed, any other action is seen, under the given conditions, to have been impossible. Now we saw that both these assertions were equally meaningless, and that they also involved a false conception of duration.

Nevertheless it will be worth while to dwell on this latter form of the determinist argument, even though it be only to explain from our point of view the meaning of the two words " determination " and " causality." In vain do we argue that there cannot be any question either of foreseeing a future action in the way that an astronomical phenomenon is foreseen, or of asserting, when once an action is done, that any other action would have been impossible under the given conditions. In vain do we add that, even when it takes this form : " The same causes produce the same effects," the principle of universal determination loses every shred of meaning in the inner world of conscious states. The determinist will perhaps

Analysis of the conception of cause, which underlies the whole determinist argument.

yield to our arguments on each of these three
points in particular, will admit that in the psychical field one cannot ascribe any of these three
meanings to the word determination, will probably
fail to discover a fourth meaning, and yet will go
on repeating that the act is inseparably bound
up with its antecedents. We thus find ourselves
here confronted by so deep-seated a misapprehen-
sion and so obstinate a prejudice that we cannot
get the better of them without attacking them at
their root, which is the principle of causality. By
analysing the concept of cause, we shall show the
ambiguity which it involves, and, though not
aiming at a formal definition of freedom, we shall
perhaps get beyond the purely negative idea of
it which we have framed up to the present.

We perceive physical phenomena, and these
phenomena obey laws. This means : (1) that

Causality as "regular suc-cession" does not apply to conscious states and cannot dis-prove free will. phenomena *a, b, c, d,* previously perceived, can occur again in the same
shape ; (2) that a certain phenomenon
P, which appeared after the conditions
a, b, c, d, and after these conditions
only, will not fail to recur as soon as the
same conditions are again present. If the principle of causality told us nothing more, as the empiricists claim, we should willingly grant these
philosophers that their principle is derived from
experience ; but it would no longer prove anything
against our freedom. For it would then be understood that definite antecedents give rise to a

definite consequent *wherever* experience shows us
this regular succession ; but the question is
whether this regularity is found in the domain
of consciousness too, and that is the whole problem of free will. We grant you for a moment
that the principle of causality is nothing but the
summing up of the uniform and unconditional
successions observed in the past : by what right,
then, do you apply it to those deep-seated states
of consciousness in which no regular succession
has yet been discovered, since the attempt to
foresee them ever fails ? And how can you base
on this principle your argument to prove the
determinism of inner states, when, according
to you, the determinism of observed facts is
the sole source of the principle itself ? In truth,
when the empiricists make use of the principle
of causality to disprove human freedom, they take
the word cause in a new meaning, which is the
very meaning given to it by common sense.

To assert the regular succession of two phenomena is, indeed, to recognize that, the first being
given, we already catch sight of the second. But
this wholly subjective connexion between two ideas
is not enough for common sense. It seems to
common sense that, if the idea of the second
phenomenon is already implied in that of the first,
the second phenomenon itself must exist objectively, in some way or other, within the first phenomenon. And common sense was bound to come
to this conclusion, because to distinguish exactly

between an objective connexion of phenomena and a subjective association between their ideas presupposes a fairly high degree of philosophical culture. We thus pass imperceptibly from the first meaning to the second, and we picture the causal relation as a kind of prefiguring of the future phenomenon in its present conditions. Now this prefiguring can be understood in two very different ways, and it is just here that the ambiguity begins.

In the first place, mathematics furnishes us with *one* type of this kind of prefiguring. The very movement by which we draw the circumference of a circle on a sheet of paper generates all the mathematical properties of this figure : in this sense an unlimited number of theorems can be said to pre-exist within the definition, although they will be spread out in duration for the mathematician who deduces them. It is true that we are here in the realm of pure quantity and that, as geometrical properties can be expressed in the form of equations, it is easy to understand how the original equation, expressing the fundamental property of the figure, is transformed into an unlimited number of new ones, all virtually contained in the first. On the contrary, physical phenomena, which succeed one another and are perceived by our senses, are distinguished by quality not less than by quantity, so that there would be some difficulty in at once declaring them

Causality, as the prefiguring of the future phenomenon in its present conditions, in one form destroys concrete phenomena.

equivalent to one another. But, just because
they are perceived through our sense-organs, we
seem justified in ascribing their qualitative differences to the impression which they make on us and
in assuming, behind the heterogeneity of our sensations, a homogeneous physical universe. Thus,
we shall strip matter of the concrete qualities
with which our senses clothe it, colour, heat, resistance, even weight, and we shall finally find
ourselves confronted with homogeneous extensity,
space without body. The only step then remaining will be to describe figures in space, to make
them move according to mathematically formulated laws, and to explain the apparent qualities
of matter by the shape, position, and motion of
these geometrical figures. Now, position is given
by a system of fixed magnitudes and motion is
expressed by a law, i.e. by a constant relation
between variable magnitudes ; but shape is a
mental image, and, however tenuous, however
transparent we assume it to be, it still constitutes,
in so far as our imagination has, so to speak, the
visual perception of it, a concrete and therefore
irreducible quality of matter. It will therefore
be necessary to make a clean sweep of this image
itself and replace it by the abstract formula of the
movement which gives rise to the figure. Picture then algebraical relations getting entangled
in one another, becoming objective by this very
entanglement, and producing, by the mere effect
of their complexity, concrete, visible, and tangible

reality,—you will be merely drawing the consequences of the principle of causality, understood
in the sense of an actual prefiguring of the future
in the present. The scientists of our time do not
seem, indeed, to have carried abstraction so far,
except perhaps Lord Kelvin. This acute and profound physicist assumed that space is filled with
a homogeneous and incompressible fluid in which
vortices move, thus producing the properties of
matter : these vortices are the constituent elements of bodies ; the atom thus becomes a movement, and physical phenomena are reduced to
regular movements taking place within an incompressible fluid. But, if you will notice that this
fluid is perfectly homogeneous, that between its
parts there is neither an empty interval which
separates them nor any difference whatever by
which they can be distinguished, you will see that
all movement taking place within this fluid is
really equivalent to absolute immobility, since
before, during, and after the movement nothing
changes and nothing has changed in the whole.
The movement which is here spoken of is thus not
a movement which actually takes place, but only
a movement which is pictured mentally : it is a
relation between relations. It is implicitly supposed, though perhaps not actually realized, that
motion has something to do with consciousness,
that in space there are only simultaneities, and
that the business of the physicist is to provide
us with the means of calculating these relations

of simultaneity for any moment of our duration. Nowhere has mechanism been carried further than in this system, since the very shape of the ultimate elements of matter is here reduced to a movement. But the Cartesian physics already anticipated this interpretation ; for if matter is nothing, as Descartes claimed, but homogeneous extensity, the movements of the parts of this extensity can be conceived through the abstract law which governs them or through an algebraical equation between variable magnitudes, but cannot be represented under the concrete form of an image. And it would not be difficult to prove that the more the progress of mechanical explanations enables us to develop this conception of causality and therefore to relieve the atom of the weight of its sensible qualities, the more the concrete existence of the phenomena of nature tends to vanish into algebraical smoke.

Thus understood, the relation of causality is a necessary relation in the sense that it will indefinitely approach the relation of identity, as a curve approaches its asymptote. The principle of identity is the absolute law of our consciousness :　it asserts that what is thought is thought at the moment when we think it : and what gives this principle its absolute necessity is that it does not bind the future to the present, but only the present to the present : it expresses the unshakable confidence that consciousness feels in

It thus leads to Descartes' physics and Spinoza's metaphysics, but cannot bind future to present without neglecting duration.

itself, so long as, faithful to its duty, it confines itself to declaring the apparent present state of the mind. But the principle of causality, in so far as it is supposed to bind the future to the present, could never take the form of a necessary principle ; for the successive moments of real time are not bound up with one another, and no effort of logic will succeed in proving that what has been will be or will continue to be, that the same antecedents will always give rise to identical consequents. Descartes understood this so well that he attributed the regularity of the physical world and the continuation of the same effects to the constantly renewed grace of Providence ; he built up, as it were, an instantaneous physics, intended for a universe the whole duration of which might as well be confined to the present moment. And Spinoza maintained that the indefinite series of phenomena, which takes for us the form of a succession in time, was equivalent, in the absolute, to the divine unity : he thus assumed, on the one hand, that the relation of apparent causality between phenomena melted away into a relation of identity in the absolute, and, on the other, that the indefinite duration of things was all contained in a single moment, which is eternity. In short, whether we study Cartesian physics, Spinozistic metaphysics, or the scientific theories of our own time, we shall find everywhere the same anxiety to establish a relation of logical necessity between cause and effect, and we shall see that this anxiety shows itself in a tendency to transform relations of succession into relations of inherence, to do away with active duration, and to substitute for apparent causality a fundamental identity.

Now, if the development of the notion of causality, understood in the sense of necessary connexion, leads to the Spinozistic or Cartesian conception of nature, inversely, all relation of necessary determination established between successive phenomena may be supposed to arise from our perceiving, in a confused form, some mathematical mechanism behind their heterogeneity. We do not claim that common sense has any intuition of the kinetic theories of matter, still less perhaps of a Spinozistic mechanism ; but it will be seen that the more the effect seems necessarily bound up with the cause, the more we tend to put it in the cause itself, as a mathematical consequence in its principle, and thus to cancel the effect of duration. That under the influence of the same external conditions I do not behave to-day as I behaved yesterday is not at all surprising, because I *change*, because I *endure*. But things considered apart from our perception do not seem to endure ; and the more thoroughly we examine this idea, the more absurd it seems to us to suppose that the same cause should not produce to-day the effect which it produced yesterday. We certainly feel, it is true, that although things do not

The necessary determination of phenomena implies non-duration ; but we endure and are therefore free.

P

endure as we do ourselves, nevertheless there must be some reason why phenomena are seen to *succeed* one another instead of being set out all at once. And this is why the notion of causality, although it gets indefinitely near that of identity, will never seem to us to coincide with it, unless we conceive clearly the idea of a mathematical mechanism or unless some subtle metaphysics removes our very legitimate scruples on the point. It is no less obvious that our belief in the necessary determination of phenomena by one another becomes stronger in proportion as we are more inclined to regard duration as a subjective form of our consciousness. In other words, the more we tend to set up the causal relation as a relation of necessary determination, the more we assert thereby that things do not *endure* like ourselves. This amounts to saying that the more we strengthen the principle of causality, the more we emphasize the difference between a physical series and a psychical one. Whence, finally, it would result (however paradoxical the opinion may seem) that the assumption of a relation of mathematical inherence between external phenomena ought to bring with it, as a natural or at least as a plausible consequence, the belief in human free will. But this last consequence will not concern us for the moment : we are merely trying here to trace out the first meaning of the word causality, and we think we have shown that the prefiguring of the future in the present is easily conceived under a mathematical form, thanks to a certain conception of duration which, without seeming to be so, is fairly familiar to common sense.

But there is a prefiguring of another kind, still more familiar to our mind, because immediate

Prefiguring, as having an idea of a future act which we cannot realize without effort, does not involve necessary determination. consciousness gives us the type of it. We go, in fact, through successive states of consciousness, and although the later was not contained in the earlier, we had before us at the time a more or less confused idea of it. The actual realization of this idea, however, did not appear as certain but merely as possible. Yet, between the idea and the action, some hardly perceptible intermediate processes come in, the whole mass of which takes for us a form *sui generis*, which is called the feeling of effort. And from the idea to the effort, from the effort to the act, the progress has been so continuous that we cannot say where the idea and the effort end, and where the act begins. Hence we see that in a certain sense we may still say here that the future was prefigured in the present ; but it must be added that this prefiguring is very imperfect, since the future action of which we have the present idea is conceived as realizable but not as realized, and since, even when we plan the effort necessary to accomplish it, we feel that there is still time to stop. If, then, we decide to picture the causal relation in this second form, we can assert *a priori* that there will no longer be a relation of necessary determination between the cause and the effect, for the effect will no longer be given in the cause. It will be there only in the state of pure possibility and as a vague idea which perhaps will not be followed by the corresponding action. But we shall not be surprised that this approximation is enough for common sense if we think of the readiness with which children and primitive people accept the idea of a whimsical Nature, in which caprice plays a part no less important than necessity. Nay, this way of conceiving causality will be more easily understood by the general run of people, since it does not demand any effort of abstraction and only implies a certain analogy between the outer and the inner world, between the succession of objective phenomena and that of our subjective states.

In truth, this second way of conceiving the relation of cause to effect is more natural than the first in that it immediately satisfies the need This second conception of of a mental image. If we look for the causality leads to Leibniz as phenomenon B within the phenomenon the first led A, which regularly precedes it, the reason to Spinoza. is that the habit of associating the two images ends in giving us the idea of the second phenomenon wrapped up, as it were, in that of the first. It is natural, then, that we should push this objectification to its furthest limit and that we should make the phenomenon A itself into a psychic state, in which the phenomenon B is supposed to be contained as a very vague idea. We simply suppose, thereby, that the objective connexion of the two phenomena resembles the subjective association which suggested the idea of it to us. The qualities of things are thus set up as actual *states*, somewhat analogous to those of our own self ; the material universe is credited with a vague personality which is diffused through space and which, although not exactly endowed with a con-scious will, is led on from one state to another by an inner impulse, a kind of effort. Such was ancient hylozoism, a half-hearted and even con-tradictory hypothesis, which left matter its exten-sity although attributing to it real conscious states, and which spread the qualities of matter through-out extensity while treating these qualities as inner i.e. simple states.   It was reserved for Leibniz to do away with this contradiction and to show that, if the succession of external qualities or phenomena is understood as the succession of our own ideas, these qualities must be regarded as simple states or perceptions, and the matter which supports them as an unextended monad, analogous to our soul.   But, if such be the case, the successive states of matter cannot be per-ceived from the outside any more than our own psychic states ; the hypothesis of pre-established harmony must be introduced in order to explain how these inner states are representative of one another.   Thus, with our second conception of the relation of causality we reach Leibniz, as with the first we reached Spinoza.   And in both cases we merely push to their extreme limit or formulate

with greater precision two half-hearted and confused ideas of common sense.

Now it is obvious that the relation of causality,
understood in this second way, does not involve
the necessary determination of the effect
by the cause. History indeed proves it.
We see that ancient hylozoism, the first
outcome of this conception of causality, explained
the regular succession of causes and effects by a
real *deus ex machina* : sometimes it was a Necessity
external to things and hovering over them, sometimes an inner Reason acting by rules somewhat
similar to those which govern our own conduct.
Nor do the perceptions of Leibniz's monad neces-
sitate one another ; God has to regulate their order
in advance.   In fact, Leibniz's determinism does
not spring from his conception of the monad, but
from the fact that he builds up the universe with
monads only.   Having denied all mechanical
influence of substances on one another, he had to
explain how it happens that their states correspond.   Hence a determinism which arises from
the necessity of positing a pre-established harmony,
and not at all from the dynamic conception of
the relation of causality.   But let us leave
history aside.   Consciousness itself testifies that
the abstract idea of force is that of indeter-
minate effort, that of an effort which has not
yet issued in an act and in which the act is
still only at the stage of an idea.   In other
words, the dynamic conception of the causal

relation ascribes to things a duration absolutely like our own, whatever may be the nature of this duration ; to picture in this way the relation of cause to effect is to assume that the future is not more closely bound up with the present in the external world than it is in our own inner life.

It follows from this twofold analysis that the principle of causality involves two contradictory conceptions of duration, two mutually exclusive ways of prefiguring the future in the present. Sometimes all phenomena, physical or psychical, are pictured as *enduring* in the same way, and therefore in the way that *we* do : in this case the future will exist in the present only as an idea, and the passing from the present to the future will take the form of an effort which does not always lead to the realization of the idea conceived. Sometimes, on the other hand, duration is regarded as the characteristic form of conscious states ; in this case, things are no longer supposed to *endure* as we do, and a mathematical pre-existence of their future in their present is admitted. Now, each of these two hypotheses, when taken by itself, safeguards human freedom ; for the first would lead to the result that even the phenomena of nature were contingent, and the second, by attributing the necessary determination of physical phenomena to the fact that things do not *endure* as we do, invites us to regard the self which is subject to duration

Each of these contradictory interpretations of causality and duration by itself safeguards freedom ; taken together they destroy it.

as a free force. Therefore, every clear conception of causality, where we know our own meaning, leads to the idea of human freedom as a natural consequence. Unfortunately, the habit has grown up of taking the principle of causality in both senses at the same time, because the one is more flattering to our imagination and the other is more favourable to mathematical reasoning. Sometimes we think particularly of the regular *succession* of physical phenomena and of the kind of inner effort by which one *becomes* another ; sometimes we fix our mind on the absolute *regularity* of these phenomena, and from the idea of regularity we pass by imperceptible steps to that of mathematical necessity, which excludes duration understood in the first way. And we do not see any harm in letting these two conceptions blend into one another, and in assigning greater importance to the one or the other according as we are more or less concerned with the interests of science. But to apply the principle of causality, in this ambiguous form, to the succession of conscious states, is uselessly and wantonly to run into inextricable difficulties. The idea of force, which really excludes that of necessary determination, has got into the habit, so to speak, of amalgamating with that of necessity, in consequence of the very use which we make of the principle of causality in nature. On the one hand, we know force only through the witness of consciousness, and consciousness does not assert, does not even understand, the absolute determination, now, of actions that are still to come : that is all that experience teaches us, and if we hold by experience we should say that we feel ourselves free, that we perceive force, rightly or wrongly, as a free spontaneity. But, on the other hand, this idea of force, carried over into nature, travelling there side by side with the idea of necessity, has got corrupted before it returns from the journey. It returns impregnated with the idea of necessity : and in the light of the rôle which we have made it play in the external world, we regard force as determining with strict necessity the effects which flow from it. Here again the mistake made by consciousness arises from the fact that it looks at the self, not directly, but by a kind of refraction through the forms which it has lent to external perception, and which the latter does not give back without having left its mark on them. A compromise, as it were, has been brought about between the idea of force and that of necessary determination. The wholly mechanical determination of two external phenomena by one another now assumes in our eyes the same form as the dynamic relation of our exertion of force to the act which springs from it : but, in return, this latter relation takes the form of a mathematical derivation, the human action being supposed to issue mechanically, and therefore necessarily, from the force which produces it. There is no doubt that this mingling of two different and almost opposite ideas offers advantages to common sense, since it enables us to picture in the same way, and denote by one and the same word, both the relation which exists between two moments of our life and that which binds together the successive moments of the external world. We have seen that, though our deepest conscious states exclude numerical multiplicity, yet we break them up into parts external to one another ; that though the elements of concrete duration permeate one another, duration expressing itself in extensity exhibits moments as distinct as the bodies scattered in space. Is it surprising, then, that between the moments of our life, when it has been, so to speak, objectified, we set up a relation analogous to the objective relation of causality, and that an exchange, which again may be compared to the phenomenon of endosmosis, takes place between the dynamic idea of free effort and the mathematical concept of necessary determination ?

But the sundering of these two ideas is an accomplished fact in the natural sciences. The physicist **Though united** may speak of *forces*, and even picture **in popular** their mode of action by analogy with an **thought, the** **ideas of free** inner effort, but he will never introduce **effort and ne-** this hypothesis into a scientific explana- **cessary deter-** **mination are** tion. Even those who, with Faraday, **kept apart** **by physical** replace the extended atoms by dynamic **science.** points, will treat the centres of force and the lines of force mathematically, without troubling about force itself considered as an activity or an effort. It thus comes to be understood that the relation of external causality is purely mathematical, and has no resemblance to the relation between psychical force and the act which springs from it.

It is now time to add that the relation of inner causality is purely dynamic, and has no analogy **They should** with the relation of two external phe- **be kept apart,** nomena which condition one another. **too, by psychology.** For, as the latter are capable of recurring in a homogeneous space, their relation can be expressed in terms of a law, whereas deep-seated psychic states occur once in consciousness and will never occur again. A careful analysis of the psychological phenomenon led us to this conclusion in the beginning : the study of the notions of causality and duration, viewed in themselves, has merely confirmed it.

We can now formulate our conception of freedom. Freedom is the relation of the concrete self to the act which it performs. This **Freedom real but indefin-** relation is indefinable, just because we **able.** *are* free. For we can analyse a thing, but not a process; we can break up extensity, but not duration. Or, if we persist in analysing it, we unconsciously transform the process into a thing and duration into extensity. By the very fact of breaking up concrete time we set out its moments in homogeneous space ; in place of the doing we put the already done ; and, as we have begun by, so to speak, stereotyping the activity of the self, we see spontaneity settle down into inertia and freedom into necessity. Thus, any positive definition of freedom will ensure the victory of determinism.

Shall we define the free act by saying of this act, when it is once done, that it might have been left undone ? But this assertion, as also its opposite, implies the idea of an absolute equivalence between concrete duration and its spatial symbol : and as soon as we admit this equivalence, we are led on, by the very development of the formula which we have just set forth, to the most rigid determinism.

Shall we define the free act as " that which could not be foreseen, even when all the conditions were known in advance ? " But to conceive all the conditions as given, is, when dealing with concrete duration, to place oneself at the very moment at which the act is being performed. Or else it is admitted that the matter of psychic duration can be pictured symbolically in advance, which amounts, as we said, to treating time as a homogeneous medium, and to reasserting in new words the absolute equivalence of duration with its symbol. A closer study of this second definition of freedom will thus bring us once more to determinism.

Shall we finally define the free act by saying that it is not necessarily determined by its cause ? But either these words lose their meaning or we understand by them that the same inner causes will not always call forth the same effects. We admit, then, that the psychic antecedents of a free act can be repeated, that freedom is displayed in a duration whose moments resemble one another, and that time is a homogeneous medium, like space. We shall thus be brought back to the idea of an equivalence between duration and its spatial symbol ; and by pressing the definition of freedom which we have laid down, we shall once more get determinism out of it.

To sum up ; every demand for explanation in regard to freedom comes back, without our suspecting it, to the following question : " Can time be adequately represented by space ? " To which we answer : Yes, if you are dealing with time flown ; No, if you speak of time flowing. Now, the free act takes place in time which is flowing and not in time which has already flown. Freedom is therefore a fact, and among the facts which we observe there is none clearer. All the difficulties of the problem, and the problem itself, arise from the desire to endow duration with the same attributes as extensity, to interpret a succession by a simultaneity, and to express the idea of freedom in a language into which it is obviously untranslatable.

CONCLUSION

To sum up the foregoing discussion, we shall put aside for the present Kant's terminology and also his doctrine, to which we shall return later, and we shall take the point of view of common sense. Modern psychology seems to us particularly concerned to prove that we perceive things through the medium of certain forms, borrowed from our own constitution. This tendency has become more and more marked since Kant : while the German philosopher drew a sharp line of separation between time and space, the extensive and the intensive, and, as we should say to-day, consciousness and external perception, the empirical school, carrying analysis still further, tries to reconstruct the extensive out of the intensive, space out of duration, and externality out of inner states. Physics, moreover, comes in to complete the work of psychology in this respect : it shows that, if we wish to forecast phenomena, we must make a clean sweep of the impression which they produce on consciousness and treat sensations as signs of reality, not as reality itself.

It seemed to us that there was good reason to set ourselves the opposite problem and to ask **But are not the states of the self perceived through forms borrowed from the external world?** whether the most obvious states of the ego itself, which we believe that we grasp directly, are not mostly perceived through the medium of certain forms borrowed from the external world, which thus gives us back what we have lent it. *A priori* it seems fairly probable that this is what happens. For, assuming that the forms alluded to, into which we fit matter, come entirely from the mind, it seems difficult to apply them constantly to objects without the latter soon leaving a mark on them : by then using these forms to gain a knowledge of our own person we run the risk of mistaking for the colouring of the self the reflection of the frame in which we place it, i.e. the external world. But one can go further still and assert that forms applicable to things cannot be entirely our own work, that they must result from a compromise between matter and mind, that if we give much to matter we probably receive something from it, and that thus, when we try to grasp ourselves after an excursion into the external world, we no longer have our hands free.

Now just as, in order to ascertain the real relations of physical phenomena to one another, we abstract whatever obviously clashes with them in our way of perceiving and thinking, so, in order to view the self in its original purity, psychology ought to eliminate or correct certain forms which bear the obvious mark of the external world. What are these forms? When isolated from one another and regarded as so many distinct units, psychic states seem to be more or less *intense*. Next, looked at in their multiplicity, they unfold in time and constitute *duration*. Finally, in their relations to one another, and in so far as a certain unity is preserved throughout their multiplicity, they seem to *determine* one another. Intensity, duration, voluntary determination, these are the three ideas which had to be clarified by ridding them of all that they owe to the intrusion of the sensible world and, in a word, to the obsession of the idea of space.

To understand the intensity, duration and voluntary determination of psychic states, we must eliminate the idea of space.

Examining the first of these ideas, we found that psychic phenomena were in themselves pure quality or qualitative multiplicity, and that, on the other hand, their cause situated in space was quantity. In so far as this quality becomes the sign of the quantity and we suspect the presence of the latter behind the former, we call it intensity. The intensity of a simple state, therefore, is not quantity but its qualitative sign. You will find that it arises from a compromise between

Intensity is quality and not quantity or magnitude.

pure quality, which is the state of consciousness, and pure quantity, which is necessarily space. Now you give up this compromise without the least scruple when you study external things, since you then leave aside the forces themselves, assuming that they exist, and consider only their measurable and extended effects. Why, then, do you keep to this hybrid concept when you analyse in its turn the state of consciousness ? If magnitude, outside you, is never intensive, intensity, within you, is never magnitude. It is through having overlooked this that philosophers have been compelled to distinguish two kinds of quantity, the one extensive, the other intensive, without ever succeeding in explaining what they had in common or how the same words " increase " and " decrease " could be used for things so unlike. In the same way they are responsible for the exaggerations of psychophysics, for as soon as the power of increasing in magnitude is attributed to sensation in any other than a metaphorical sense, we are invited to find out by how much it increases. And, although consciousness does not measure intensive quantity, it does not follow that science may not succeed indirectly in doing so, if it be a magnitude. Hence, either a psychophysical formula is possible or the intensity of a simple psychic state is pure quality.

Turning then to the concept of multiplicity, we saw that to construct a number we must first have the intuition of a homogeneous medium,

Q

viz. space, in which terms distinct from one another could be set out in line, and, secondly, a process of permeation and organization by which these units are dynamically added together and form what we called a qualitative multiplicity. It is owing to this dynamic process that the units *get added*, but it is because of their presence in space that they remain *distinct*. Hence number or discrete multiplicity also results from a compromise. Now, when we consider material objects in themselves, we give up this compromise, since we regard them as impenetrable and divisible, i.e. endlessly distinct from one another. Therefore, we must give it up, too, when we study our own selves. It is through having failed to do so that associationism has made many mistakes, such as trying to reconstruct a psychic state by the addition of distinct states of consciousness, thus substituting the symbol of the ego for the ego itself.

Our conscious states not a discrete multiplicity.

These preliminary considerations enabled us to approach the principal object of this work, the analysis of the ideas of duration and voluntary determination.

What is duration within us ? A qualitative multiplicity, with no likeness to number ; an organic evolution which is yet not an increasing quantity ; a pure heterogeneity within which there are no distinct qualities. In a word, the moments of inner duration are not external to one another.

Inner duration is a qualitative multiplicity.

What duration is there existing outside us? The present only, or, if we prefer the expression, simultaneity. No doubt external things change, but their moments do not *succeed* one another, if we retain the ordinary meaning of the word, except for a consciousness which keeps them in mind. We observe outside us at a given moment a whole system of simultaneous positions; of the simultaneities which have preceded them nothing remains. To put duration in space is really to contradict oneself and place succession within simultaneity. Hence we must not say that external things *endure*, but rather that there is in them some inexpressible reason in virtue of which we cannot examine them at successive moments of our own duration without observing that they have changed. But this change does not involve succession unless the word is taken in a new meaning: on this point we have noted the agreement of science and common sense.

In the external world we find not duration but simultaneity.

Thus in consciousness we find states which succeed, without being distinguished from one another; and in space simultaneities which, without succeeding, are distinguished from one another, in the sense that one has ceased to exist when the other appears. Outside us, mutual externality without succession; within us, succession without mutual externality.

Here again a compromise comes in. To the simultaneities, which constitute the external

world, and, although distinct, succeed one another *for our consciousness*, we attribute
succession *in themselves*. Hence the
idea that things *endure* as we do ourselves and that time may be brought
within space. But while our consciousness
thus introduces succession into external things,
inversely these things themselves externalize the
successive moments of our inner duration in
relation to one another. The simultaneities of
physical phenomena, absolutely distinct in the
sense that the one has ceased to be when the other
takes place, cut up into portions, which are also
distinct and external to one another, an inner life
in which succession implies interpenetration, just
as the pendulum of a clock cuts up into distinct
fragments and spreads out, so to speak, lengthwise, the dynamic and undivided tension of the
spring. Thus, by a real process of endosmosis
we get the mixed idea of a measurable time,
which is space in so far as it is homogeneity, and
duration in so far as it is succession, that is to
say, at bottom, the contradictory idea of succession in simultaneity.

Now, these two elements, extensity and duration, science tears asunder when it undertakes
the close study of external things.
For we have pointed out that science
retains nothing of duration but simultaneity, and nothing of motion itself
but the position of the moving body,

i.e. immobility. A very sharp separation is here made and space gets the best of it.

Therefore the same separation will have to be made again, but this time to the advantage of duration, when inner phenomena are studied, —not inner phenomena once developed, to be sure, or after the discursive reason has separated them and set them out in a homogeneous medium in order to understand them, but inner phenomena in their developing, and in so far as they make up, by their interpenetration, the continuous evolution of a free person. Duration, thus restored to its original purity, will appear as a wholly qualitative multiplicity, an absolute heterogeneity of elements which pass over into one another.

Now it is because they have neglected to make this necessary separation that one party has been **The neglect to separate extensity and duration leads one party to deny freedom and the other to define it.** led to deny freedom and the other to define it, and thereby, involuntarily, to deny it too. They ask in fact whether the act could or could not be foreseen, the whole of its conditions being given ; and whether they assert it or deny it, they admit that this totality of conditions could be conceived as given in advance : which amounts, as we have shown, to treating duration as a homogeneous thing and intensities as magnitudes. They will either say that the act is *determined* by its conditions, without perceiving that they are playing on the double sense of the word causality, and that they are thus giving to duration at the same time two forms which are mutually exclusive. Or else they will appeal to the principle of the conservation of energy, without asking whether this principle is equally applicable to the moments of the external world, which are equivalent to one another, and to the moments of a living and conscious being, which acquire a richer and richer content. In whatever way, in a word, freedom is viewed, it cannot be denied except on condition of identifying time with space; it cannot be defined except on condition of demanding that space should adequately represent time; it cannot be argued about in one sense or the other except on condition of previously confusing succession and simultaneity. All determinism will thus be refuted by experience, but every attempt to define freedom will open the way to determinism.

Inquiring then why this separation of duration and extensity, which science carries out so naturally in the external world, demands such an effort and rouses so much repugnance when it is a question of inner states, we were not long in perceiving the reason. The main object of science is to forecast and measure: now we cannot forecast physical phenomena except on condition that we assume that they do not *endure* as we do ; and, on the other hand, the only thing we are able to measure is space. Hence the breach here comes about of itself between quality and quantity, between true

This separation favourable to physical science, but against the interests of language and social life.

duration and pure extensity. But when we turn to our conscious states, we have everything to gain by keeping up the illusion through which we make them share in the reciprocal externality of outer things, because this distinctness, and at the same time this solidification, enables us to give them fixed names in spite of their instability, and distinct ones in spite of their interpenetration. It enables us to objectify them, to throw them out into the current of social life.

Hence there are finally two different selves, one of which is, as it were, the external projection of the other, its spatial and, so to speak, social representation. We reach the former by deep introspection, which leads us to grasp our inner states as living things, constantly *becoming*, as states not amenable to measure, which permeate one another and of which the succession in duration has nothing in·common with juxtaposition in homogeneous space. But the moments at which we thus grasp ourselves are rare, and that is just why we are rarely free. The greater part of the time we live outside ourselves, hardly perceiving anything of ourselves but our own ghost, a colourless shadow which pure duration projects into homogeneous space. Hence our life unfolds in space rather than in time; we live for the external world rather than for ourselves; we speak rather than think; we "are acted" rather than act ourselves. To act

Hence two different selves: (1) the fundamental self: (2) its spatial and social representation : only the former is free.

freely is to recover possession of oneself, and to get back into pure duration.

Kant's great mistake was to take time as a homogeneous medium. He did not notice that real duration is made up of moments inside one another, and that when it seems to assume the form of a homogeneous whole, it is because it gets expressed in space. Thus the very distinction which he makes between space and time amounts at bottom to confusing time with space, and the symbolical representation of the ego with the ego itself. He thought that consciousness was incapable of perceiving psychic states otherwise than by juxtaposition, forgetting that a medium in which these states are set side by side and distinguished from one another is of course space, and not duration. He was thereby led to believe that the same states can recur in the depths of consciousness, just as the same physical phenomena are repeated in space ; this at least is what he implicitly admitted when he ascribed to the causal relation the same meaning and the same function in the inner as in the outer world. Thus freedom was made into an incomprehensible fact. And yet, owing to his unlimited though unconscious confidence in this inner perception whose scope he tried to restrict, his belief in freedom remained unshakable. He therefore raised it to the sphere of noumena ; and as he had

Kant clung to freedom, but put the self which is free outside both space and time.

confused duration with space, he made this genuine free self, which is indeed outside space, into a self which is supposed to be outside duration too, and therefore out of the reach of our faculty of knowledge. But the truth is that we perceive this self whenever, by a strenuous effort of reflection, we turn our eyes from the shadow which follows us and retire into ourselves. Though we generally live and act outside our own person, in space rather than in duration, and though by this means we give a handle to the law of causality, which binds the same effects to the same causes, we can nevertheless always get back into pure duration, of which the moments are internal and heterogeneous to one another, and in which a cause cannot repeat its effect since it will never repeat itself.

In this very confusion of true duration with its symbol both the strength and the weakness **Kant regarded** of Kantianism reside. Kant imagines **both time and** on the one side "things in themselves," **space as ho-** **mogeneous.** and on the other a homogeneous Time and Space, through which the "things in themselves," are refracted : thus are supposed to arise on the one hand the phenomenal self—a self which consciousness perceives—and, on the other, external objects. Time and space on this view would not be any more in us than outside us ; the very distinction of outside and inside would be the work of time and space. This doctrine has the advantage of providing our empirical thought with a solid foundation, and of guaranteeing that phenomena, as phenomena, are adequately knowable. Indeed, we might set up these phenomena as absolute and do without the incomprehensible "things in themselves," were it not that the Practical Reason, the revealer of duty, came in, like the Platonic reminiscence, to warn us that the "thing in itself" exists, invisible but present. The controlling factor in the whole of this theory is the very sharp distinction between the matter of consciousness and its form, between the homogeneous and the heterogeneous, and this vital distinction would probably never have been made unless time also had been regarded as a medium indifferent to what fills it.

But if time, as immediate consciousness perceives it, were, like space, a homogeneous medium, **But if time, as duration, were homogeneous, science could deal with it.** science would be able to deal with it, as it can with space. Now we have tried to prove that duration, as duration, and motion, as motion, elude the grasp of mathematics : of time everything slips through its fingers but simultaneity, and of movement everything but immobility. This is what the Kantians and even their opponents do not seem to have perceived : in this so-called phenomenal world, which, we are told, is a world cut out for scientific knowledge, all the relations which cannot be translated into simultaneity, i.e. into space, are scientifically unknowable.

In the second place, in a duration assumed to

be homogeneous, the same states could occur over again, causality would imply neces-

And freedom would be incomprehensible. Kant's solution. sary determination, and all freedom would become incomprehensible. Such, indeed, is the result to which the Critique of Pure Reason leads. But instead of concluding from this that real duration is heterogeneous, which, by clearing up the second difficulty, would have called his attention to the first, Kant preferred to put freedom outside time and to raise an impassable barrier between the world of phenomena, which he hands over root and branch to our understanding, and the world of things in themselves, which he forbids us to enter.

But perhaps this distinction is too sharply drawn and perhaps the barrier is easier to cross than he supposed. For if perchance

How corrected by taking real duration into account. the moments of real duration, perceived by an attentive consciousness, permeated one another instead of lying side by side, and if these moments formed in relation to one another a heterogeneity within which the idea of necessary determination lost every shred of meaning, then the self grasped by consciousness would be a free cause, we should have absolute knowledge of ourselves, and, on the other hand, just because this absolute constantly commingles with phenomena and, while filling itself with them, permeates them, these phenomena themselves would not be as amenable as is claimed to mathematical reasoning.

So we have assumed the existence of a homogeneous Space and, with Kant, distinguished this space from the matter which fills it. With him we have admitted that homogeneous space is a "form of our sensibility": and we understand by this simply that other minds, e.g. those of animals, although they perceive objects, do not distinguish them so clearly either from one another or from themselves. This intuition of a homogeneous medium, an intuition peculiar to man, enables us to externalize our concepts in relation to one another, reveals to us the objectivity of things, and thus, in two ways, on the one hand by getting everything ready for language, and on the other by showing us an external world, quite distinct from ourselves, in the perception of which all minds have a common share, foreshadows and prepares the way for social life.

With Kant, we assume a homogeneous space, the intuition of which is peculiar to man and prepares the way for social life.

Over against this homogeneous space we have put the self as perceived by an attentive consciousness, a living self, whose states, at once undistinguished and unstable, cannot be separated without changing their nature, and cannot receive a fixed form or be expressed in words without becoming public property. How could this self, which distinguishes external objects so sharply and represents them so easily by means of symbols, withstand the temptation to introduce the same distinctions into its own life and to replace the

But if concrete duration is heterogeneous, the relation of psychic state to act is unique and the act is rightly judged free.

interpenetration of its psychic states, their wholly qualitative multiplicity, by a numerical plurality of terms which are distinguished from one another, set side by side, and expressed by means of words ? In place of a heterogeneous duration whose moments permeate one another, we thus get a homogeneous time whose moments are strung on a spatial line. In place of an inner life whose successive phases, each unique of its kind, cannot be expressed in the fixed terms of language, we get a self which can be artificially reconstructed, and simple psychic states which can be added to and taken from one another just like the letters of the alphabet in forming words. Now, this must not be thought to be a mode of symbolical representation only, for immediate intuition and discursive thought are one in concrete reality, and the very mechanism by which we only meant at first to explain our conduct will end by also controlling it. Our psychic states, separating then from each other, will get solidified ; between our ideas, thus crystallized, and our external movements we shall witness permanent associations being formed ; and little by little, as our consciousness thus imitates the process by which nervous matter procures reflex actions, automatism will cover over freedom.[1] It is just at this point

[1] Renouvier has already spoken of these voluntary acts which may be compared to reflex movements, and he has restricted freedom to moments of crisis. But he does not seem to have noticed that the process of our free activity goes

that the associationists and the determinists come
in on the one side, and the Kantians on the other.
As they look at only the commonest aspect of
our conscious life, they perceive clearly marked
states, which can recur in time like physical
phenomena, and to which the law of causal determination applies, if we wish, in the same sense as
it does to nature. As, on the other hand, the
medium in which these psychic states are set side
by side exhibits parts external to one another,
in which the same facts seem capable of being
repeated, they do not hesitate to make time a
homogeneous medium and treat it as space.
Henceforth all difference between duration and
extensity, succession and simultaneity, is abolished:
the only thing left is to turn freedom out of doors,
or, if you cannot entirely throw off your traditional
respect for it, to escort it with all due ceremony
up to the supratemporal domain of " things in themselves," whose mysterious threshold your consciousness cannot cross. But, in our view, there is a third
course which might be taken, namely, to carry

on, as it were, unknown to ourselves, in the obscure depths of
our consciousness at every moment of duration, that the very
feeling of duration comes from this source, and that without
this heterogeneous and continuous duration, in which our self
evolves, there would be no moral crisis. The study, even the
close study, of a given free action will thus not settle the problem of freedom. The whole series of our heterogeneous
states of consciousness must be taken into consideration. In
other words, it is in a close analysis of the idea of duration
that the key to the problem must be sought.

ourselves back in thought to those moments of our life when we made some serious decision, moments unique of their kind, which will never be repeated —any more than the past phases in the history of a nation will ever come back again. We should see that if these past states cannot be adequately expressed in words or artificially reconstructed by a juxtaposition of simpler states, it is because in their dynamic unity and wholly qualitative multiplicity they are phases of our real and concrete duration, a heterogeneous duration and a living one. We should see that, if our action was pronounced by us to be free, it is because the relation of this action to the state from which it issued could not be expressed by a law, this psychic state being unique of its kind and unable ever to occur again. We should see, finally, that the very idea of necessary determination here loses every shred of meaning, that there cannot be any question either of foreseeing the act before it is performed or of reasoning about the possibility of the contrary action once the deed is done, for to have all the conditions given is, in concrete duration, to place oneself at the very moment of the act and not to foresee it. But we should also understand the illusion which makes the one party think that they are compelled to deny freedom, and the others that they must define it. It is because the transition is made by imperceptible steps from concrete duration, whose elements permeate one another, to symbolical duration, whose moments are set side by side, and consequently from free activity to conscious automatism. It is because, although we are free whenever we are willing to get back into ourselves, it seldom happens that we are willing. It is because, finally, even in the cases where the action is freely performed, we cannot reason about it without setting out its conditions externally to one another, therefore in space and no longer in pure duration. The problem of freedom has thus sprung from a misunderstanding : it has been to the moderns what the paradoxes of the Eleatics were to the ancients, and, like these paradoxes, it has its origin in the illusion through which we confuse succession and simultaneity, duration and extensity, quality and quantity.

Just Beautiful.

INDEX

pared to musical phrase, 127;
consciousness compared to invisible
musician, 147.

Nativist theory of space, 93.

Nature beauty in, 14; compared
with art, 16; profoundly utilitarian, 33; view taken by mechanism and dynamism, 140 f.; concrete phenomena of, abolished,
207; view of, as whimsical, 212.

Necessity, see also Determinism:
mechanism cannot escape, 140;
as *deus ex machina* in ancient
hylozoism, 214; and idea of force,
216 ff.

Neiglick, his photometric experiments, 52

Noël, G., article on number and space,
75 *n.*

Notes, why classified as higher and
lower, 45 f.

Noumenon, freedom as, 232.

Novelist, how effects produced, 133,
164, 185.

Number, natural series, 2, 80; definition of, 75; article on space and,
75 *n.*; units of, identical, 76;
units of, distinct, 77, 226; implies
intuition of space, 77 ff., 83 f., 225;
both unit and synthesis of units,
80 f.; discontinuity of, 82; process of forming a, 82 f.; why divisible at will, 83; subjective and
objective in, 84; thought of as a
juxtaposition, 85; inapplicable to
multiplicity of conscious states, 87;
and impenetrability of matter,
89; those in daily use have
emotional equivalents, 123; time
as a, 195, 197; results from a compromise, 226.

Objective, definition of, 83.

Objectivity, of things, 236.

Objects, contrasted with progress,
111, 112, 219; can be analysed,
112; help to cut up our psychic
life, 124 f.; seem to live and grow
old, 130; tend to fix changing
feelings, 130; in human soul
processes, not, 131.

Order, of succession, implies space,
101 f.

Pain, and pity, 18 f.; as sign of
future reaction, 33; intensity of,
35 f.; Darwin on, 37; conceived as
distinct thing, 159.

Paradox, the Eleatic, 74, 112 f., 240.

Parallelism, of physical and psychical
series, 146 f.

Paralysis, and feeling of effort, 21, 22.

Past, no recurrence of, 154, 200 f.,
219, 232, 233, 239.

Paul, his prediction of Peter's action,
184 ff.

Pendulum, counting oscillations of,
104 f.; what do oscillations of,
measure, 107 ff; oscillations of,
help to cut up our psychic life,
109; spreads out undivided tension of spring, 228.

Permeation, see Interpenetration.

Peter, Paul's prediction of his
action, 184 ff.

Photometric experiments, 52 ff.

Physics, and sound-vibrations, 46;
and degrees of luminous intensity,
52 f.; interested in external
cause, 71; physical phenomena
and law, 202; Cartesian, 207, 208;
Descartes' instantaneous, 208; and
forecasting of phenomena, 222, 230.

Pillon, F., article on number and
space, 75 *n.*

Pitch, of a sound, 44 f.

Plateau, his method of measuring
luminous sensations, 56.

Plato, quoted, 168; Platonic reminiscence, 234.

Pleasure, as sign of future reaction,
33 f.; and bodily inclination, 38;
keenness of, as inertia of organism,
38; conceived as distinct thing, 159.

Poetry, how effects produced, 15.

"Possible acts," 174 f., 239.

Postulate, Delbœuf's, 60; Fechner's,
60; fundamental, of psychophysics,
65, 70; underlying geometrical
representation of voluntary activity, 179.

Prediction, astronomical, 117, 192 ff.,
198; determinism and, 173, 183 ff.,
220; real duration and, 183 ff.; of
future actions, 183 ff., 229, 239;
probable and infallible, 183 f., and
character, 184, 172; hypothetical
case of Peter and Paul, 184 ff.;
all foreseeing as seeing, 195, 197,
198; of phenomena, and physics,
222, 230.

Prefiguring, of future phenomenon in
present conditions, 204 ff., 210;
two kinds of, 204 ff., 215; as in
mathematics, 204 f.; as having
idea of possible future act, 211 f.

Pressure, sensation of, 47 f.

Process, motion as a, 111; conscious
states not things but, 131, 196;
misleading to substitute material
symbol for, 190; cannot be
analysed, 219.

Progress, motion as a, 111; not

116, 193 ff. ; **attempts to do away with** duration and causality, 208 f. ; separates ideas of free effort and necessary determination, 218 ; attempts to measure intensive quantity, 225 ; separates extensity and duration, 228, 230 ; main object of, 230 ; could deal with time if homogeneous, 234.

Scottish philosophers, **72.**

Sculpture, ancient, 15.

Self, whole, reflected in each conscious state, 98, 165 ; recovery of the fundamental, 100, 128, 129, 231, 233, 236, 240 ; introduces distinctions derived from external objects into its own states, 109, 125, 237 ; superficial, with mutually external states, 125, 128, 136, 138, 167, 237 ; deep-seated, with interpenetrating states, 125, 128, 136, 164, 236 ; many conscious states never blend with whole mass of, 135, 166, 168 ; perceived by refraction through space, 128, 129, 137, 167, 183, 217, 223 ; the two aspects of the, 129 ff., 137, 231 ; tendency to form secondary, **138,** 166 ; not an association of terms, 139, 159 ff., 164, 165, 226 ; recourse to living and concrete, necessary to solve problems of causality, freedom, etc., 139 ; activity of, cannot be compared to that of any other force, 143, 216 ; perception of, through forms borrowed from external world, 154, 217, 223 ; self-determination, 165 ; parasitic, as result of education, 166 ; free decisions spring from whole or fundamental, 167, 172, 231, 240 ; covered over with crust of clean-cut psychic states, 167 ; does not intervene in carrying out every-day acts, 168 ; uprush of deep-seated, at moment of crisis, 169 ; distinction of psychic states leads to mechanical conception of, 171 ; constantly changing and growing, 171, 175 f. ; view of, involved in geometrical representation of process of deciding, 176 f. ; infallible in affirming its immediate experiences, 183 ; as a free force, 216, 235 ; Kant put free, outside space and duration, **233 ;** Kant and phenomenal, 233 ; as a free cause, 235.

Sensations, intensity of, 1 ff., 7 ff., 20 ff., 40, 42, 47, 72 f. ; art yielding only, **17 ;** and external causes, 20 ff. ; peripheral, and muscular effort, 24, 26 ; peripheral, and

violent emotions, **31 ;** magnitude of, 31, 32, 47, 72 ; affective and representative : affective, 32 ff., 72 f. ; and organic disturbance, 32 f. ; pleasure and pain, 33 ff. ; affective, and free movements, **33 ;** representative, 39 ff., 73, 90 ; medium, 41 ; representative, measured by external causes, 42 ; of sound, 43 f. ; of heat and cold, 46 f., 64 ; of pressure and weight, 47 f. ; increase of, and sensation of increase, 48 ; as quantity or quality, 48 ; of movement, 50 ; of light, 50 ff. ; measurement of luminous, 52 ff. ; psychophysics attempts to measure, 55 ff., 62, 63, 225 ; equal and identical, 57, 62, 63, 64, 69 ; law connecting stimulus and, 60 f. ; as quantities, 62, 65, 66 ; addition of, 64 ; considered as a sum, 65, 67 ; how quantitative differences set up between, 71 f. ; as pure quality, 72 ; and space, 92, 93, 95 ; can space be built up from, 94 ; simultaneous and identical, 95 ; of motion, indivisible, 112 ; influence of language on, 131 ; not objects but processes, 131 ; altered by repetition, 131 ; physics treats, as signs of reality, 223.

Series, natural, of numbers, 2, 80 ; double aspect of each term in a, 124, 226 ; physical and psychical, 210.

" Several," use of, implies space, **122.**

Shape, as quality of matter, 205.

Simplicity, different senses of, in dynamism and mechanism, 141.

Simultaneity, implies space, 95 ; measuring duration and counting, 108 f. ; as connecting link between space and duration, 110 ; definition of, 110 ; in measuring velocity, 114, 117 ; used in defining equal intervals of time, 116, 119 ; in space nothing but, 116, 206, 227 ; and astronomical prediction, 116 f., 193 ff. ; dealt with by mathematics, 119 ; attempted representation of succession by, 180, 221 ; all relations not translatable into, are scientifically unknowable, 234.

Sleep, and perception of duration, 126.

Smell, illustration from associations of, 161 f.

Social life, self with well-defined states better adapted to, 128, 137, 139, 167, 231 ; more important